Our Feeling Universe

An exploration

of the

Universal Feeling Body

A catalogue record for this book is available from the British Library

ISBN: 978-1-907962-72-1

Publication Date: September 2024

Published by Cranmore Publications

Exeter, England

cranpubs@gmail.com

Pondering the nature of the Universe

Have you ever thought about the nature of the Universe? It is very easy to get caught up in day-to-day human activities and routines, and not to spend much time pondering such a lofty issue. Of course, throughout the ages those of a philosophical disposition have spent ample time considering this issue and they have come up with a plethora of diverse proposals concerning both the nature of the Universe, and the limits of what we can possibly know. Two of the views that have been espoused are that the Universe is wholly comprised of water, and that the Universe isn't comprised of anything because it doesn't exist.

An elegant and very appealing view is that the Universe exists but that humans are cognitively barred from being able to come to know its true nature. This is a view that should be taken extremely seriously. According to this line of thought, humans are prisoners who are forever constrained by the world of perceptions. We perceive, and carry out scientific experiments on, that which we know not what. The issue is: How could one possibly have conclusive evidence, irrefutable truth, concerning the true nature of that which underpins one's perceptions?

There is undoubtedly a chasm: there is the Universe in its unobserved state; there is the Universe that is observed. Our prime concern in that which follows is to consider, and explore, the nature of the Universe in its unobserved state. There is thus an underlying and inevitable optimism that it is possible for humans to escape the prison of their perceptions and come to know the true nature of the Universe.

Three false views

False view 1: Some humans believe that the entire Universe is imbued with a force that is so vibrant that it makes sense to assert: 'the Universe is alive'. According to this view, the entire Universe is a living entity.

False view 2: Some humans believe that the entire Universe is pervaded with consciousness or psyche/mind.

False view 3: Some humans have an extremely dull view of the Universe. These humans see the Universe as being largely, or wholly, comprised of 'dead' stuff; not 'dead' as opposed to 'living', but 'dead' in terms of being devoid of any vibrancy, of any agency, of any feeling. A 'dead' Universe is conceived of as a mechanism that is constituted out of 'matter', out of 'physical stuff', which moves in accordance with physical laws.

A fresh start

Let us start afresh.

A speck of thought/awareness in a feeling Universe

My objective is to help you to see that the three views that I have just outlined are all false. In that which follows I will be introducing you to the nature of the Universe in its unobserved state. In so doing, I realise that what to me is blindingly apparent, is for you merely a proposal for your consideration.

Let us begin. The Universe as a whole is not a living entity, and it is not pervaded with consciousness or psyche/mind. Yet, the Universe is not a mechanism that is constituted out of 'matter'. The entire Universe is pervaded with, and is fundamentally constituted by, feeling. You are a speck of thought/awareness, and the Universe is your feeling body. The Universe in its unobserved state can aptly be referred to as the Universal Feeling Body.

The mind-body problem and the concept of 'mind'

You are probably well aware of what has been dubbed 'the mind-body problem' – the issue of how the human 'mind' relates to the human body. The main reason that this problem is so intractable is the very widespread assumption that the Universe is overwhelmingly devoid of feeling. Such an assumption naturally leads to the belief that one's human body, as part of the Universe, is devoid of feeling, and that feeling must exist in a different realm – a realm that has been called 'mind'. In this way, a chasm has been created between two conceptual realms: the realm of human body / 'matter', and the realm of 'mind'/feeling.

As soon as one comes to appreciate that the Universal Feeling Body is one's body, then one can see that this conceptual chasm between two realms does not exist. There are just specks of thought/awareness that come into and out of existence, and every one of these specks has the Universal Feeling Body as its body. If one seeks to give an account of everything that exists in the Universe, then one has no need for the concept of 'mind', and one also has no need for the concept of 'matter'.

I am a speck of thought/awareness, therefore I am

Descartes famously asserted: "I think, therefore I am". He was right. Of course he was right. Let us assert: "I am a speck of thought/awareness, therefore I am". If one is not aware, then one cannot assert anything.

What is this 'I' that I am? This 'I' is a speck of thought/awareness; nothing more; nothing less. To talk of 'you', to talk of there being an 'I', is to talk of there being a speck of thought/awareness. Yet, a speck of thought/awareness has a close travelling companion, and this companion is its animal body. Every animal body is unique. In our exploration of the Universal Feeling Body, we will consider both that which is you, and that which is your unique travelling companion.

The currant bun

Imagine a currant bun: a bun that has currants scattered throughout its inside. Imagine that this bun is the Universal Feeling Body. Imagine that the currants are specks of thought/awareness. When a human body, or the body of another animal, loses its speck of thought/awareness, then there is no entity that is differentiated from the Universal Feeling Body. The 'I' that existed no longer exists; the currant that was in the bun has disappeared, but the bun still exists. If a particular human body, or non-human animal body, regains their speck of thought/awareness, then an 'I' exists. A currant has emerged in the bun.

Thought/awareness is a singular entity

Thought and awareness do not come apart. They are tightly coupled bedfellows. Thought is a phenomenon that requires awareness. There cannot be thinking – a process of thought – if there is not awareness of the previous thought. There cannot be a single thought in the absence of the awareness of its existence. Conversely, whilst one can imagine that awareness could exist in the absence of thought, this is an anomaly, an unnatural and transitory state. Where there is awareness, thought is continuously pressing at the gates, trying to barge its way in, as if it were a battering ram being perpetually bashed into a door.

Thought/awareness is one. It is a singular entity.

Computation

One might believe that thought can exist without awareness. If so, then one actually has in mind computation. Computation is carried out by computers, and is also carried out by brains in the absence of a speck of thought/awareness. Computation is a complex movement pattern.

When there is no speck of thought/awareness in an animal body, then the brain in that body is engaging in computation. When there is a speck of thought/awareness in an animal body, then the brain in that body engages in computations that the speck of thought/awareness never becomes aware of.

Awareness cannot exist without thought

One might believe that awareness can exist without thought. Indeed, one might have temporarily experienced these states oneself. However, this is a mirage. Consider the assertion that a human body needs to breathe in order to be alive. One could object to this assertion by saying that it is false because one has held one's breath for a minute, and that during this time one's human body was not breathing, but one's human body was alive. Therefore, one could assert that a human body can be alive without breathing. Whilst this might strictly be true – your human body was both not breathing and alive – it is a bizarre assertion to make. It is much more sensible to assert that a human body needs to breathe in order to be alive.

In a human body, breathing and aliveness do not come apart; they are tightly coupled bedfellows. In a similar vein, one needs to assert that thought/awareness is a singular entity; there are not two phenomena here that can sensibly be separated. More than this, this singular entity is what delineates one within the Universal Feeling Body. This entity constitutes that which is an 'I'; an entity that is aware of its surroundings and is thus opposed to its surroundings. These surroundings include both the animal body in which it intermittently emerges and the wider whole that is the Universal Feeling Body.

I am a speck of thought/awareness, therefore I am.

What we think, we become

The Buddha wisely asserted that: "What we think, we become". This can be rephrased as: 'Thought becomes thought'. One thought leads to another thought. Of course, thought/awareness is the real phenomenon here. So, we have: 'thought/awareness becomes thought/awareness'. We are specks of thought/awareness that are situated within a Universal Feeling Body. Anything that happens within that Universal Feeling Body has the potential to intrude upon, and change the direction of, a process of thought/awareness.

'Thought/awareness becomes thought/awareness'. This is not an insular activity. Even if one isolates oneself in a monastery, in the wilderness, in self-confinement, one's Universal Feeling Body will impinge on the process of thought/awareness becoming thought/awareness.

We are what we feel

A speck of thought/awareness is an 'I'; it is what differentiates one from the Universal Feeling Body. An 'I' is set against, opposed to, the Universe. An 'I' is also in a state of perennial becoming; for, 'thought/awareness becomes thought/awareness'. Yet, there are two sides to us. The currant is situated within a bun. We are specks of thought/awareness, but these specks have a Universal Feeling Body. We are, fundamentally, what we feel. The bun is more important, more fundamental, than the currant.

What we feel, we become

We could assert: 'I feel, therefore I am'. But this really won't do. 'I feel' is sufficient. However, 'I feel, therefore the Universe feels', is more informative.

We could assert: 'What we feel, we become'. This is true. Very true. This isn't just true; it is of essential importance to fully comprehend what this means. For, whilst the 'I' that is one is created by a speck of thought/awareness, that which defines one as an individual, in terms of who and what one actually is, is grounded in the feelings of one's human body. To talk of what defines one as an individual, is to talk of the nature of a particular segment of the Universe.

What we feel, we become.

The origin of thought in feeling

Where do our thoughts come from? Why do we have the particular thoughts that we have? Why does a process of thought/awareness go off in a particular direction? When one seeks answers to these questions one will always ultimately end up in the realm of feelings, the realm of the Universal Feeling Body.

Specks of thought/awareness emerge in animal brains

Try and envision the Universe as a totality. You can then try to envision a segment, any segment, of this totality. In so doing, you should come to appreciate that this segment is a unique collection of feelings. Envision a particular speck of thought/awareness emerging; it has the Universal Feeling Body as its body. However, this speck is also, inevitably, located in a specific location, a particular segment of the Universe. Specks of thought/awareness emerge in the brains of animals. A brain, and the rest of the body of an animal, is a specific location that is a unique collection of feelings.

The observed Universe

As a speck of thought/awareness, one becomes aware of a world that is not one: the observed Universe. The observed Universe contains 'parts': the objects that one visually perceives. The Universal Feeling Body is that which underpins that which one visually perceives. The Universal Feeling Body is not constituted out of 'parts', it is constituted out of 'things'. 'Things' are defined by their feeling states. 'Things' have an observer-independent existence; in contrast, 'parts' are delineated by an observer. The 'parts' that are visually perceived are themselves states of feeling. Every object that one visually perceives is feeling. However, one cannot visually perceive 'things'; and, one cannot visually perceive feelings.

The matrix of feeling that is the Universal Feeling Body – the unobserved Universe – is the home which specks of thought/awareness emerge within. These specks come into and out of existence, but they cannot be observed. That which creates and beholds the observed Universe cannot itself be observed.

The Universal Feeling Body, the unobserved Universe, the observed Universe, and the Universe

Let us be clear on the distinction between these terms: the 'Universal Feeling Body', 'the unobserved Universe', 'the observed Universe', and the 'Universe'. I am using the terms 'the unobserved Universe' and the 'Universal Feeling Body' interchangeably; for, I am seeking to get you to appreciate that 'the unobserved Universe' is the 'Universal Feeling Body'. Strictly, the term 'the unobserved Universe' simply refers to the fundamental nature of the Universe, whatever that nature is. And, the term the 'Universal Feeling Body' is my term to refer to the nature of 'the unobserved Universe'. If one believed that 'the unobserved Universe' was comprised of tomatoes, then one might well use the term: the 'Universal Tomato Body'.

To say that the 'Universal Feeling Body' is 'the unobserved Universe' isn't to say that it doesn't exist when there are observers. Rather, *the use of the term is describing the fundamental nature of the Universe irrespective of whether or not it is observed.* To talk of 'the unobserved Universe' is important because the fundamental nature of the Universe does not reveal itself to observation.

Let us now consider 'the observed Universe'. This term refers to the world which visually appears to a speck of thought/awareness. This is, inevitably, a boundaried world, a world of divisions, a world of distinct objects.

The term 'Universe' refers simultaneously to both 'the unobserved Universe' and 'the observed Universe'. There is scope for potential confusion here. For, the term 'Universe' is commonly used to refer solely to the world that visually appears to a speck of thought/awareness. If one is just referring to this world of boundaries/divisions, with no regard to its underpinning 'Universal Feeling Body', then the appropriate term to use is 'the observed Universe'.

The observed Universe is comprised of 'parts' – the objects that are visually perceived.

The unobserved Universe / the Universal Feeling Body is comprised of 'things' – connections/bonds between feelings. Feelings become associated/embedded with other feelings and thereby create networks of feelings. Each of these networks is a 'thing'.

If one is referring to a portion of the Universe, this portion will contain 'things', and if this portion is observed it will also contain 'parts', be a 'part', or be a component of a 'part'. A portion of the Universe can be referred to as a 'segment'.

The chasm in the Universal Feeling Body and the segregation of the animal body

When there are no specks of thought/awareness in animal bodies, then there are no divisions in the Universal Feeling Body. When a speck of thought/awareness exists, then a division exists within the Universal Feeling Body; for, an entity exists, an 'I', which is segregated from, and set against, the rest of the Universal Feeling Body. This division creates a chasm within the Universal Feeling Body.

This chasm in the Universal Feeling Body has its inevitable counterpart in the observed Universe. For, a speck of thought/awareness inevitably creates the *appearance of a chasm* in its observed Universe. A speck of thought/awareness takes its animal body to be a part, an object, which is set against, which is segregated from, all of the other parts/objects in its observed Universe. This segregation of the animal body entails a speck of thought/awareness conceptualising its animal body as a distinct entity, as a body that is its body, and even as a body that is itself, a body that is opposed to all that is not-itself. However, this is a mirage; there is no chasm here. The real body of a speck of thought/awareness is its Universal Feeling Body.

The two bodies of a speck of thought/awareness

A speck of thought/awareness, encouraged by the visual sense of its animal body, segregates its animal body and takes it to be a distinct boundaried entity.

The fundamental body of a speck of thought/awareness is its Universal Feeling Body. We need to explore this in more detail. We can say that a speck of thought/awareness is an 'I' and that every 'I' has a unique Universal Feeling Body. For, every speck of thought/awareness has a different location, and thereby is a unique access point to the Universal Feeling Body. So, to say that every speck of thought/awareness has the Universal Feeling Body as its body, is not to say that every speck of thought/awareness has the same Universal Feeling Body.

Every speck of thought/awareness has both a unique animal body and a unique Universal Feeling Body.

What is a feeling?

What it is to be a feeling is to feel, and a feeling doesn't feel itself, it feels that which is not itself, and thereby becomes itself.

What is a node of feeling?

To say that the Universal Feeling Body is comprised of feelings, is to say that it is comprised of nodes of feeling. A node of feeling is a location at which a feeling originates. A feeling only exists for a moment, then it morphs into a new feeling. In contrast, nodes of feeling persist through time. So, Feeling^x exists in Node^1 at Time^1. Then, at Time^2, Feeling^y exists in Node^1.

The rule of association/embeddedness

There is a general rule: *every feeling in the Universal Feeling Body is increasingly affected by, and determined by, that which it is increasingly associated with.*

Association is jointly determined by space and time. Closer spatial proximity between two nodes of feeling increases their association. And, increasing time spent in closer spatial proximity also increases the association between two nodes of feeling. In addition, it will be fruitful for us to utilise the notion of embeddedness. *For two nodes of feeling to be increasingly associated is for them to be more deeply embedded.* The terms 'association' and 'embeddedness' can be used interchangeably.

Increasing association between two nodes of feeling entails deepening embeddedness. And, feelings that are more deeply embedded feel each other more intensely. Conversely, lessening association between two nodes of feeling entails decreasing embeddedness. And, feelings that are less deeply embedded feel each other less intensely. Another useful term is 'bond'; bonds between nodes of feeling can get stronger or weaker. We can also talk about a changing 'connection' between two nodes of feeling. A deeper connection is a stronger bond, which entails increasing association and deepening embeddedness.

This rule applies to the feelings in the Universal Feeling Body. However, it also applies to the parts in an observed Universe; for, these parts are constituted out of feelings. However, whilst one can talk of two parts becoming more deeply embedded, or less deeply embedded, this is an extremely crude extrapolation from what is occurring. For, bonds of association/embeddedness exist between nodes of feeling, not between the parts that are visually perceived in an observed Universe.

What is a thing?

We need to explore the nature of a thing. Things are constituted out of bonds between nodes of feeling. Every feeling in the Universal Feeling Body simultaneously partially constitutes an immense plethora of things. This is because feelings feel each other and thereby become connected to each other in a multitude of different degrees.

To become connected is to become associated/embedded, and then to either become more deeply embedded, or less deeply embedded. Every unique bundle of feeling connections is a thing. Every moment, as a ginormous multitude of new associations of nodes of feeling are formed – both strengthening associations and weakening associations – by movements in space, and by the passage of time, new connections of feelings emerge; new things emerge.

A thing is not an island; it is not something that is easily locatable and separable from its surroundings; it is not like a baby in its mother's womb. When we talk of a 'baby' and a 'womb' we are in the realm of the observed Universe of parts. Whereas, our exploration of the underlying fundamental nature of reality – the Universal Feeling Body – is an exploration of the unobserved Universe.

A thing is an association of feelings within the Universal Feeling Body. A particular thing is not something that one can sensibly attach a label, a word, to. A thing isn't anything like a 'tree', a 'pencil', or a 'dog'. A thing doesn't exist at a discrete location; it is a feeling connection between nodes of feeling that each have their own discrete location; but as the feelings fuse to form a thing, the notion of discreetness vanishes. Things are constituted out of feelings that are dispersed, yet connected; connected in such an intimate way that the many becomes one.

What distinguishes one thing from another thing? If a feeling participates in a plethora of things, why isn't this plethora of things simply one thing? The distinguisher of things is the level of embeddedness between feelings. When a group of feelings are equally embedded with each other, then this group will constitute a thing. So, when a feeling is deeply embedded with a group of other feelings, this group will be a thing. This same feeling will also be weakly embedded with another group of feelings, and this group will be another thing. This is putting it extremely simplistically; for, there is a sliding scale of embeddedness, an immense multitude of degrees of embeddedness, which means that a feeling will participate in an immense plethora of things. In other words, a feeling will participate in an immense number of deeply embedded things, an immense number of weakly embedded things, and an immense number of mediumly embedded things.

The feelings in a thing are equally embedded with each other. What this means is that they all feel each other to the same level of intensity. The feelings all feel each other deeply, weakly, or somewhere in between. Some things are tiny, and some things are massive. For instance, a tiny thing could be wholly located within what in my observed Universe I call 'the tooth of an animal'; and, a massive thing could incorporate what I call 'the Moon' and 'the Earth'.

Envision the Moon circling the Earth. Feeling connections exist between the circling Moon and the Earth below. Massive things exist. As the Moon circles around the Earth, new things are continuously forged between the Moon and the area of the Earth that is currently below the Moon. New things are forged, and some things are unforged. When the Moon is above a particular area of the Earth, the animals that exist in this area will participate in the massive things that are forged that incorporate the Moon and this area of the Earth. So, some of the feelings in the tooth of one such animal will participate in a tiny thing, and they will also simultaneously participate in massive things. The feelings in this tooth will also participate in a plethora of other 'medium-sized' things; both things which are wholly within the body of the animal in which the tooth is located, and things which extend outside of this animal body into its surroundings.

We have seen that a thing is delineated by the level of embeddedness between a collection of feelings. We have also seen that there are tiny things and massive things. Is there a connection here? Yes, because there is a strong tendency for small things to be deeply embedded, and for massive things to be weakly embedded. Smaller things tend to be much more highly associated than massive things primarily because of the close spatial proximity of the feelings. However, this is only a tendency; for, larger things can be more deeply embedded than smaller things, due to prolonged temporal duration outweighing increased spatial distance.

So, the Universal Feeling Body is constituted out of nodes of feeling, and every node has differentially embedded feeling connections with other nodes. Furthermore, any change in this network of feeling associations, whether simply the passage of a moment in time, or a change in spatial location, destroys some things, and creates new things. The individual feelings that constitute a thing simultaneously constitute lots of other things – tiny things, medium-sized things, and massive things. This means that things spatially overlay, overlap, underlay, each other. In general, weakly embedded larger things overlay/overlap/underlay, more deeply embedded smaller things.

We have conceptualised things as being entities that are in a continuous state of flux – being perennially destroyed and created. This isn't the whole story. In one sense, a particular thing only exists for the tiniest possible fragment of time, and then it turns into another thing; for, the feelings within things are continuously changing. And, not only this, but things are typically continuously gaining nodes of feeling and losing nodes of feeling.

Yet, in another sense, a particular thing can last for immense periods of time; we are talking about millions of years, and longer. For, whilst the nature of a thing in terms of the qualities of its feelings continuously changes, the thing itself in terms of the existence of the bonds between the nodes of feeling can persist.

Furthermore, whilst a particular thing might get a bit larger, or a bit smaller, or might maintain its size whilst acquiring some feelings and losing others, if the central core of the thing remains intact, then it can sensibly be said that the thing still exists. This is analogous to asserting that a particular human body still exists when its hair has grown, or when its toenails have been clipped. Such a human body, like a thing that has acquired or lost some nodes of feeling, is simultaneously different and the same.

What is a part?

We have explored what it is to be a thing. If you envision any part in your observed Universe, you can appreciate that this part will be participating in an immense plethora of things. But, what, exactly, is a part in your observed Universe? A part in an observed Universe is whatever is visually perceived and taken to be an object. More than this, a part is what a speck of thought/awareness has conceptually moulded into an object.

So, an 'apple' is a part in my observed Universe. A 'sausage' is a part in my observed Universe. A 'horse' is a part in my observed Universe. A 'horse's leg' is a part in my observed Universe. 'Totnes Castle' is a part in my observed Universe. A 'seahorse' is a part in my observed Universe. A 'ladybird' is a part in my observed Universe. A 'rainbow' is a part in my observed Universe. A 'tree' is a part in my observed Universe. A 'deer' is a part in my observed Universe. The 'Moon' is a part in my observed Universe. A 'human finger' is a part in my observed Universe. A 'human hand' is a part in my observed Universe. A 'window' is a part in my observed Universe. A 'cloud' is a part in my observed Universe. And, 'Looe Island' is a part in my observed Universe.

Anything that is visually sensed and conceptualised as an object is a part in one's observed Universe. All of these parts will be participating in an immense plethora of things. From the perspective of a speck of thought/awareness, a part in its observed Universe is a 'concept'. Whereas, from the deeper perspective of the unobserved Universe, a 'concept' is a subjective and arbitrary division/boundary within that which is undivided/boundaryless. For, there are no boundaries between feelings, and there are no boundaries between things.

The nature of feeling radiation

The Universal Feeling Body is a matrix which is characterised by feelings feeling each other: feelings feeling feelings. Every time a feeling feels another feeling, a connection, a bond, is formed. The two nodes of feeling become associated, become embedded, with each other. And, equally-embedded feelings fuse into a thing.

The more embedded that two feelings are, the more deeply they will feel each other. There are very deeply embedded things. And, there are very weakly embedded things. More than this, there is a sliding scale of embeddedness, of depth of co-feeling, between these two extremes. The more embedded that two feelings are, the greater is the depth of their feeling that they radiate between each other.

The feelings within a thing all feel each other to the same degree. A useful expression to refer to this co-feeling is 'feeling radiation'. This expression highlights the fact that when a feeling arises it is instantly felt throughout all of the things in which it participates. The instant radiation of feeling throughout things is at the heart of the Universal Feeling Body.

New feelings are continuously arising throughout the Universal Feeling Body, and are thus continuously radiating throughout their things. When a new feeling arises, it arises in a particular location, in a particular node of feeling, and it participates in the same things as the feeling that it morphed out of. For, things are forged out of nodes of feeling. This means that a new feeling arises within pre-existing things.

A new feeling makes its mark, is felt, throughout all of the things in which it participates. Furthermore, it makes a unique mark in each of its things; for, the making of such a unique mark is what distinguishes the participants of one thing, from the participants of another thing. The making of such a mark is what delineates a thing from the rest of the Universal Feeling Body. In other words, a new feeling modifies all of the feelings that participate in each of its things in a different way; for, this is precisely what it entails to participate in a thing.

As new feelings are continuously arising throughout a thing, this means that when a new feeling arises in a particular node of feeling and is instantly radiating throughout a thing, it itself is being radiated to from all of the other feelings in the thing. It becomes an open question whether it makes any sense to say that any feeling exists in any particular place, rather than it simultaneously existing in a plethora of places. For, all of the continuously arising feelings are instantly radiating throughout all of their things, and are fusing into each other throughout each of these things.

There is no doubt that at a particular moment in time, at a specific location in the Universal Feeling Body, that there will be a particular feeling. Yet, attempting to isolate such a feeling is an endeavour in abstraction, which inevitably fails to capture the continuously flowing and intermingling nature of what is occurring.

Due to the continuous instant co-radiation of feelings throughout a thing, at any moment in time a thing will have only one feeling. So, to talk of a thing, is to talk of a feeling that simultaneously exists in different locations. And, to talk of a feeling, is to talk of an entity that is simultaneously instantiated in different locations. Furthermore, all of the feelings in a thing participate in a multitude of things; so, feeling things are overlaying and underlaying each other.

The co-radiation of feeling throughout a thing means that, at any given moment in time, there is just one feeling state in a thing. Yet, every node of feeling participates in a multitude of things, an immense plethora of things, a unique collection of things. Every node of feeling in the Universal Feeling Body inevitably participates in a unique collection of things. Whilst every thing has the same feeling state throughout itself, every node of feeling has unique feeling, due to its participation in a unique collection of things.

What has just been said might seem to be contradictory. How can a thing, which is a collection of nodes of feeling, have a single feeling state throughout itself, whilst, simultaneously, the nodes of feeling themselves all have a unique feeling state? We are, for sure, entering slightly mind-boggling territory here. How this can be so can be understood if one comes to appreciate that a node of feeling radiates different depths of itself throughout each of its things. Less depths are shared in less-embedded things; greater depths are shared in increasingly embedded things. In other words, a node of feeling differentially participates in all of its things. This is why a thing has a single feeling, whereas the nodes of feeling that comprise the thing each have a unique feeling state, due to their differential participation in a unique bundle of things, an immense plethora of things which overlap and underlay each other.

The continuous process of feeling origination and feeling co-radiation throughout things continuously brings into being an immense plethora of new things. For, a new feeling brings into being a new thing. Yet, as we have already discussed, these new things are, simultaneously, slight modifications to still-existing old things.

Changing bonds = new things

Things are associations of equally-embedded feelings. Things grow in size by acquiring new feelings, and shrink by loosing feelings. For, bonds are formed between nodes of feeling and these bonds are continuously in a state of change, either becoming stronger or weaker. Any change in a bond of embeddedness between two nodes of feeling causes a thing to either grow or shrink.

Three levels of feeling and the two mini-chasms

There are three different levels of feeling intensity within the Universal Feeling Body. If you were to envision all of the feeling states that exist in the Universal Feeling Body, you could place them all on a sliding scale, a scale of how intense the feeling is. You can envision that this sliding scale has three levels of intensity within it: low-level feeling, medium-level feeling, and high-level feeling. You can then imagine that within each of these three levels some feelings will be more intense than others. For example, there will be high intensity medium-level feelings and low intensity medium-level feelings.

Whilst all of the feeling states that exist in the Universal Feeling Body could in theory be placed on a sliding scale of feeling intensity, there are also two significant thresholds, two mini-chasms, within this sliding scale. The transition from low-level feeling to medium-level feeling is a mini-chasm – a medium-level feeling feels much more intensely than a low-level feeling. Similarly, the transition from medium-level feeling to high-level feeling is a mini-chasm – a high-level feeling feels much more intensely than a medium-level feeling.

To talk of these three levels of feeling, and the two mini-chasms, is to refer to nodes of feeling origination within the Universal Feeling Body. Some bits of the Universal Feeling Body are nodes of origination of low-level feeling; some bits of the Universal Feeling Body are nodes of origination of medium-level feeling; and, some bits of the Universal Feeling Body are nodes of origination of high-level feeling.

The two mini-chasms and the three modes of the Universe

The two mini-chasms that we have just explored carve the Universe into three sections. We can refer to these three sections as the three modes of the Universe. Envision any segment of the Universe and its nature will be explicable in terms of these three modes. Mode 1 = Inanimate / Non-living. Mode 2 = Living without thought/awareness. Mode 3 = Living with thought/awareness. The two mini-chasms simultaneously delineate the intensity of the feeling that is originated in a segment of the Universe, and the mode that exists in this part of the Universe. Mode 1 = low-level feeling. Mode 2 = medium-level feeling. Mode 3 = high-level feeling.

High intensity feeling

The three different levels of feeling are bandings of feeling intensity potentiality (low-level, medium-level, and high-level). These bandings delineate the upper boundary of feeling intensity that a particular segment of the Universe can bring into existence. There are also a plethora of grades of feeling intensity within each of these bandings, some of which will actually exist at a particular moment in time. You know that feelings vary in intensity from your own experience, sometimes becoming aware of feelings that are much more intense that at other times.

From now on the term 'high intensity feeling' will be used to refer to the collection of the most intense feelings that exist within the Universal Feeling Body. This term therefore refers to the states that are the highest grades of feeling intensity within the high-level feeling banding.

Feeling origination in a tree

We can fruitfully consider the medium-level banding of feeling intensity by considering the feelings that originate in a tree. These feelings will vary through time; on some occasions they will be more intense than on other occasions. However, even the most intense feelings that are originated will not be high-level feelings, let alone high intensity feelings.

A tree can only originate medium-level feelings. A tree is a collection of nodes of origination of medium-level feelings.

The origination and radiation of feelings

I have outlined the hierarchy of feeling: the three levels of feeling (low-level, medium-level, and high-level) that exist within the Universal Feeling Body. It needs to be emphasised that these three levels concern the ability of different segments of the Universe to originate, to bring forth into existence, feelings of a particular level of intensity. This needs to be emphasised because when a feeling is brought forth into existence it instantly radiates throughout the networks of feelings – the things – which the node of feeling that originated the feeling participates in. What this means is that high-level feelings can exist in entities such as plants and fungi, and also in non-living segments of the Universe, despite these segments being unable to originate such feelings themselves. And, similarly, medium-level feelings can also exist in Mode 1 segments of the Universe.

Nodes of feeling, the three levels of feeling, and the three modes of the Universe

A fruitful way of coming to know the three levels of feeling origination, and the three modes of the Universe, is to appreciate that they are nodes of feeling. The parts of my observed Universe that I call 'animal bodies' are, in the Universal Feeling Body, nodes of origination of high-level feeling. These animal bodies are Mode 3 segments of the Universe. One could think of a particular animal body as an originator of high-level feelings, but it would be much more accurate to think of this animal body as being pervaded with nodes of high-level feeling. For, the former conception only makes sense in the observed Universe of parts; whereas, the latter conception can be applied in both the observed Universe of parts and the unobserved Universe of things.

In a similar way, one can envision those segments of the Universe that are living without thought/awareness as collections of nodes of medium-level feeling; these plants and fungi are Mode 2 segments of the Universe. And, one can envision those segments of the Universe that are non-living as collections of nodes of low-level feeling; these inanimate entities are Mode 1 segments of the Universe.

Nodes of feeling participate in things – networks of feelings. And these networks will typically contain nodes of feeling that are of different levels. In this situation, the nodes with the highest level of feeling in a thing, will dominate that thing. For, as these feelings instantly radiate throughout the thing, their greater feeling intensity will dwarf the lower intensity nodes of feeling.

Nodes of feeling and degree of embeddedness intertwine to determine the feeling intensity in a thing

We have just explored how those things which contain nodes of feeling origination from more than one level will be dominated by the nodes from the highest level. We can say a little more about this here in terms of how this relates to the different levels of embeddedness of feelings.

We have already explored how feelings that are more deeply embedded – a deeply embedded thing – feel each other more deeply than the feelings that are less deeply embedded in a less deeply embedded thing. Our question is: How does the domination of a thing by its nodes of highest level feeling intertwine with the existence of things of different degrees of embeddedness?

If we imagine a thing that contains nodes of feeling origination from all three levels, then we can envision the difference between this being a deeply embedded thing and a weakly embedded thing. In both scenarios, the thing will be dominated by the nodes of high-level feeling. Yet, there is a very important difference. If this were a deeply embedded thing, then the feelings would feel each other very deeply, which means that the thing would be pervaded with the high-level feelings that emanate from the nodes of high-level feeling. In contrast, if this were a weakly embedded thing, then as all of the feelings in the thing feel each other much less deeply, this means that although the thing is dominated by its nodes of high-level feeling, that the feeling state of the thing is much less intense than it is in the deeply embedded thing. This is because the nodes of high-level feeling are sharing/radiating much less of themselves in the weakly embedded thing.

There are two sliding scales that are intertwining in a thing: intensity of feeling originating in nodes, and degree of embeddedness. The interplay between these two sliding scales determines the level of feeling intensity in a thing. A thing which contains nodes of high-level feeling, if it has sufficiently low embeddedness, can have low-level feeling. Whereas, a thing that has only nodes of low-level and medium-level feeling will, if it is reasonably deeply embedded, have medium-level feeling.

A speck of thought/awareness is a 'qualityless window'

A speck of thought/awareness is neither a part nor a thing. A part is observable, and is delineated by an observer; whereas, a speck of thought/awareness isn't observable, and it delineates itself. A thing doesn't have a discrete location, and things are in a continuous process of creation and destruction; whereas, a speck of thought/awareness has a discrete location, and it exists for a prolonged period of time. A speck of thought/awareness is a segment of the Universe. A speck of thought/awareness is a transcender of worlds – the unobserved Universe and the observed Universe. It exists in the unobserved Universe – the Universal Feeling Body; yet it is a beholder of parts, of feelings, and of itself. It becomes aware of the feelings which constitute the Universal Feeling Body. It becomes aware of the parts, the objects, which come into being when it conceptualises/moulds the structured sensings of the visual sense. It also, inevitably, becomes aware of itself.

A speck of thought/awareness arises from some of the operations of an animal brain. A speck of thought/awareness either exists, or it doesn't exist; there are no halfway houses. It is as if there is an on-off switch; and this switch is the state of the operations of an animal brain. A speck of thought/awareness arises from a particular pattern of movement within the Universal Feeling Body. This particular movement pattern sometimes exists within those segments of the Universe that a structured visual sensing and conceptual moulding can label as 'an animal brain'. A speck of thought/awareness doesn't radiate feelings, it doesn't get feelings transmitted to it, and it doesn't contain feelings.

A speck of thought/awareness is a 'qualityless window' through which the feelings of the Universal Feeling Body appear, and through which the moulded Universe of boundaries and distinct objects is both created and viewed.

When a speck of thought/awareness exists it gets increasingly embedded with particular nodes of feeling in the Universal Feeling Body, which, in terms of the observed Universe, means that the speck gets increasingly embedded with parts. However, such embeddedness is very different to the bonds of embeddedness that are forged between feelings. When feelings get embedded with each other this involves a two-way feeling connection between the feelings: the feeling of feeling, the creation of things, and the radiation of feelings throughout these things. Whereas, when a speck of thought/awareness becomes increasingly embedded with the feeling that exists in a node of feeling, this is a one-way event which entails not the feeling of feeling, not the radiation of feeling, but the increasing awareness of the feeling that exists in the node of feeling. A speck of thought/awareness, due to weakening association, can also become less aware of the feeling that exists in a node of feeling.

A speck of thought/awareness's embeddedness with its animal body

When a speck of thought/awareness emerges it becomes increasingly embedded with particular nodes of feeling. In particular, it becomes exceedingly deeply embedded with the nodes of feeling that exist in the animal body – for example, the head, torso, arms, and legs, of a human body – which it emerges within. This is due to both the extremely close spatial proximity of these particular nodes of feeling within its Universal Feeling Body, and the increasing length of time over which this close spatial proximity exists.

Close spatial proximity, and an increasing duration of time at a close spatial proximity, are very potent instigators of increasing association. This means that a speck of thought/awareness will be the most highly associated with, most deeply embedded with, the nodes of feeling that are located in the animal body that it emerges within. Furthermore, all of the feelings that a speck of thought/awareness can possibly become aware of will be located in the things that its animal body participates in.

A speck of thought/awareness's embeddedness with its Universal Feeling Body – the awareness of feelings in the animal body that originate outside of the animal body

A speck of thought/awareness is situated within, and is engulfed by, the networks of feelings, the things, that its animal body participates in. This means that a speck of thought/awareness will become aware of feelings that originate in its animal body, and it will also become aware of feelings that exist in its animal body that originated outside of its animal body.

For, the vast majority of the things that an animal body participates in extend far beyond the boundaries of that animal body, and when a feeling originates at any location in a thing it is instantly radiated and felt throughout that thing. So, when a speck of thought/awareness becomes aware of a feeling in its animal body this feeling might have originated outside of this body.

A speck of thought/awareness cannot escape from the close travelling companion that is its animal body. What this means is that a speck of thought/awareness cannot become aware of the feelings that participate in things that its animal body does not participate in. For, wherever a speck of thought/awareness goes, its animal body goes, and its animal body will thereby participate in the things that contain the nodes of feeling that its speck of thought/awareness can become associated with.

It will be fruitful for us to explore a little further what it means for a speck of thought/awareness to become aware of the feelings in the things that its animal body participates in. A feeling originates in a particular discrete location – in a particular node of feeling – but it is instantly differentially radiated throughout the things in which that location participates. So, there are two questions. Firstly: Where did a feeling originate? Secondly: Where is this feeling felt?

The Universal Feeling Body of a speck of thought/awareness is the feelings – the nodes of feeling – that exist in all of the things that its animal body participates in. All of these feelings will be radiated into the speck of thought/awareness's animal body. Due to the extremely deep level of embeddedness between a speck of thought/awareness and its animal body, a speck of thought/awareness typically becomes aware of the feelings that exist in its animal body. When a speck of thought/awareness becomes aware of a feeling in its animal body the issue of where the feeling originated is typically not addressed by the speck of thought/awareness. For, this issue only raises itself for consideration when one realises that there is a distinction between a location of origination of a feeling and the locations where that feeling is felt.

A speck of thought/awareness's embeddedness with its Universal Feeling Body – the direct awareness of feelings that exist outside of the animal body

We have just explored how a speck of thought/awareness can become aware of feelings in its animal body that originate outside of its animal body, due to the instant radiation of feeling throughout the plethora of things that its animal body participates in. A speck of thought/awareness can also become directly aware of feelings that exist outside of its animal body. We are here talking about the direct awareness of a feeling at the location of its origination. Such awareness is possible due to the embeddedness of a speck of thought/awareness with some of the nodes of feeling that exist in its Universal Feeling Body.

The animal body of a speck of thought/awareness is a part that is created by a speck of thought/awareness. There is no real boundary between an animal body and the rest of the Universal Feeling Body. A speck of thought/awareness becomes directly aware of feelings that exist outside of its animal body in exactly the same way that it becomes aware of feelings that exist inside its animal body; it simply becomes aware of the nodes of feeling in its Universal Feeling Body that it is deeply embedded with.

A speck of thought/awareness is almost always less embedded with the nodes of feeling that exist outside of its animal body, than it is with the nodes of feeling that constitute its animal body. What are the implications of this? This lesser embeddedness outside of the animal body means that for a speck of thought/awareness to become directly aware of a feeling at a point of origination outside of its animal body that the feeling needs to be particularly intense. In turn, this means that a speck of thought/awareness typically only becomes aware of the nodes of high-level feeling that exist in other animal bodies. Furthermore, the intensity of the high-level feelings that exist within animal bodies varies through time. Times of low intensity high-level feelings are the norm, and are punctuated by moments of high intensity feelings (such as excruciating pain). When it comes to the phenomenon of becoming directly aware of feelings that exist outside of its animal body, a speck of thought/awareness typically only becomes aware of high intensity feelings. Such feelings are stark and they demand to be noticed.

Spectacles, toes, and a rabbit

We should further explore an issue that has just been raised. This is the fact that a speck of thought/awareness is almost always less embedded with nodes of feeling that exist outside of its animal body, than it is with the nodes of feeling that constitute its animal body. Our question is: What are the exceptions to this general rule?

A speck of thought/awareness is located in the brain of an animal. So, the extremities of the animal body – such as the toes of a human body – will be the bits of the animal body that are the least embedded with that body's speck of thought/awareness. Let us assume that the animal body of a speck of thought/awareness wears spectacles, and has worn the same pair of spectacles for sixteen hours a day for twenty years. Due to the much greater spatial proximity, it is easy to appreciate how the speck of thought/awareness can be more embedded with the spectacles than with the toes of its animal body. This doesn't mean that the speck of thought/awareness is more likely to become aware of the feelings in the spectacles, than the feeling in the toes! For, as we have explored, spectacles are nodes of low-level feeling.

If we were to replace the spectacles with a rabbit, we can then envision a human body that is walking around for sixteen hours a day with a rabbit sitting on one of its shoulders. In this scenario, it is quite easy for us to appreciate how the speck of thought/awareness in the human body can become more embedded with the rabbit than with the toes of its human body. Furthermore, and in contrast to the spectacles scenario, as the rabbit is a collection of nodes of high-level feeling, the speck of thought/awareness in the human body might become more aware of the feelings in the rabbit, than the feelings in the toes of its human body.

Why does a speck of thought/awareness become aware of a feeling?

We need to answer this important question: What are the factors that determine which feelings a speck of thought/awareness becomes aware of? For, the animal body is pervaded with such an immense plethora of things that a speck of thought/awareness could seemingly be continuously overwhelmed with feelings. And, on top of this, a speck of thought/awareness can reach outside of its animal body and become directly aware of feelings at their point of origination.

We have previously explored the interplay between the levels of feeling in nodes of feeling and the degree of embeddedness of things. Due to this interplay, the vast majority of the things that an animal body participates in will have medium-level feeling and low-level feeling. Why is this? The nodes of feeling that are the animal body are high-level feelings; therefore, the things that wholly exist within an animal body are things with high-level feeling. In contrast, the vast majority of the things that an animal body participates in are massive, extending way beyond the boundary of the animal body, and these things are typically overwhelmingly constituted by nodes of low-level feeling and medium-level feeling. These things also typically have a relatively low degree of embeddedness. This interplay results in the overwhelming majority of these things having either low-level feeling or medium-level feeling. This means that the overwhelming majority of the feelings that radiate into an animal body are low-level and medium-level feelings.

Let us now switch our focus to a speck of thought/awareness becoming embedded with nodes of feeling that exist outside of its close travelling companion, and thereby acquiring the potential to become directly aware of the feelings that exist in these nodes of feeling. When a speck of thought/awareness becomes embedded with some of the nodes of feeling that exist in its broader Universal Feeling Body – which is comprised of the things that its animal body participates in – the vast majority of the nodes of feeling that it is becoming embedded with are nodes of low-level feeling and medium-level feeling. This means that despite being embedded with an immense number of these nodes, that a speck will not become aware of the feelings in the vast majority of them.

A speck of thought/awareness is not continuously overwhelmed with feelings because it typically only becomes aware of high-level feelings. A speck of thought/awareness typically becomes aware of three types of feeling. Firstly, the feelings that it is most highly associated with: the high-level feelings that originate in its animal body. Secondly, the feelings in its broader Universal Feeling Body that it is embedded with and which are nodes of high-level feeling that are originating high intensity feelings; these feelings are so stark that they demand to be noticed, and they are noticed at their point of origination. Thirdly, the feelings which are radiated into its animal body via the high-level feeling things that its animal body participates in. In addition to these three types of feeling that a speck of thought/awareness typically becomes aware of, a speck of thought/awareness occasionally becomes directly aware of feelings that are not high intensity feelings at their point of origination.

Universal feeling unfoldment and the non-awareness of the feelings that are one's home

As the Universe has very gradually evolved from its relatively mundane beginnings, to the fabulous Earth of 2024, the intensity of its feeling has increased. The non-living Universe has a low-level of feeling, life-forms that lack thought/awareness (flowers, trees, fungi, etc.) have a medium-level of feeling, whilst life-forms that have thought/awareness (humans, dolphins, birds, frogs, dinosaurs, cats, dogs, cows, etc.) have a high-level of feeling.

If you are sitting at home by yourself watching television, then your immediate surroundings will be the high-level feelings that originate in your human body. These are the feelings that you are the most highly associated with. This combination of high association with high-level means that you can easily become aware of these feelings. These high-level feelings participate in the things that constitute your next nearest surroundings: your clothes and your house/home. These surroundings are constituted out of low-level feelings, along with a possible sprinkling of medium-level feelings, such as some houseplants. As it is rare for a speck of thought/awareness to become aware of non-high-level feelings, it is unlikely that you will become aware of the feelings that are your house/home. The most likely circumstances in which one might become aware of the feelings that are one's home would be if one lived in a house which has a tragic/emotionally-charged history, such as a 'haunted house'. We will explore this possibility in due course.

The Cornish pasty and the mattress – the forging and unforging of things within the Universal Feeling Body

Let us imagine that a human body walks into a supermarket and picks up a vegan Cornish pasty. In this situation the human body will become increasingly embedded with the pasty. However, if the human body puts the vegan Cornish pasty back on the shelf and walks away from it, then the embeddedness immediately starts to fade, and it fades rapidly. This is an example of the forging of weakly embedded things.

It is hard to adequately describe what is occurring here using words. To put it rather crudely, as the human body approaches the supermarket, weakly embedded things start to be forged that incorporate the human body and the supermarket. Keep in mind that in the Universal Feeling Body there are no objects/parts – there is no supermarket or human body – there are simply nodes of feeling that move in certain ways, and such movements both forge some things and erode other things. As the human body gets increasingly close to the pasty, increasing numbers of things are forged that incorporate the human body and the pasty, and the things that are forged progressively become increasingly embedded. This progression of the creation of more increasingly embedded things reaches its zenith when the human body puts the pasty back on the shelf. As the human body walks away from the pasty, the number of things that incorporate the human body and the pasty starts to fade, and the things that come into being are progressively decreasingly embedded things.

It is important to keep in mind that the attempt to describe the Universal Feeling Body using words is not an exact science. I have used the phrase 'weakly embedded things' to describe all of the things that are forged in the scenario that we have just explored. Yet, when one beholds all of the things that exist in the Universal Feeling Body, then one can see that there are an immense plethora of things that are much more weakly embedded than the things that we have just been considering in this scenario. From this perspective, all of the things that are forged in this scenario could very reasonably be called 'mediumly embedded things'.

We can now consider a different scenario which involves the forging of deeply embedded things. Imagine that two human bodies have been sleeping together on the same mattress every night, for ten hours a night, for forty years. The two human bodies will be deeply embedded with each other, and they will also each be deeply embedded with the mattress. These three segments of the Universe will jointly participate in an immense plethora of deeply embedded things. The connections have been forged over such a long period of time, and in such a close spatial proximity, that they are extremely strong. This means that the bonds will take a lot of breaking. If one of the human bodies goes to the other side of the Earth, then the bonds will hold firm; the three entities will remain participants in deeply embedded things, and they will still feel each other to almost the same extent that they did before. It will take a long period of spatial-temporal separation for these bonds to significantly fade.

The Cornish pasty, the parrot, and the mattress – the feelings that a speck of thought/awareness becomes aware of

In the previous section we used two scenarios to explore both the differential embeddedness of things, and the forging and unforging of these things. We can now utilise these two scenarios in order to explore the changing embeddedness, the changing awareness, that a speck of thought/awareness has of the feelings in its Universal Feeling Body.

In the pasty scenario, the speck of thought/awareness in the human body becomes exceptionally spatially close to the pasty. This closeness means that the speck of thought/awareness can become directly aware of the feelings in the pasty. If there were high intensity feelings in the pasty, then it is almost inevitable that the speck of thought/awareness would become directly aware of them; however, in our scenario there aren't high intensity feelings in the vegan pasty. The key point: *spatial closeness in the present moment between a speck of thought/awareness and a node of feeling enables the speck to potentially become aware of the feeling.* In our scenario, the encounter between the speck and the pasty is a transitory one, which means that the embeddedness between the pasty and the speck of thought/awareness is weak. This means that when the human body walks away from the pasty, the awareness that its speck of thought/awareness has of the nodes of feeling in this bit of its Universal Feeling Body immediately starts to fade, and this awareness fades rapidly.

In this scenario, we can imagine swapping the pasty for an animal such as a parrot. If the parrot was in extreme pain, then when the human body picks it up it is almost inevitable that its speck of thought/awareness will become directly aware of these high intensity feelings. The exceptionally close spatial proximity between the speck of thought/awareness in the human body and the parrot means that the speck becomes aware of the nodes of feeling that are the parrot's body. Indeed, the speck of thought/awareness in the human body will, in all likelihood, become directly aware of these feelings before its human body picks up the parrot. Yet, as this is a transitory encounter, as the two entities gradually move apart from each other the speck will have a rapidly decreasing awareness of the nodes of feeling that are the parrot's body.

Due to spatial-temporal separation, the speck of thought/awareness in the human body will relatively quickly become unembedded with the parrot. As the speck of thought/awareness moves through the Universal Feeling Body, it becomes increasingly aware of other bits of its Universal Feeling Body. Yet, the human body of the speck of thought/awareness remains a participant in things that encompass itself and the nodes of feeling that are the parrot's body; for, the connections that are formed by feelings feeling feelings are exceedingly long-lasting. In other words, when the embeddedness between the speck of thought/awareness in the human body and the nodes of feeling that are the parrot falls to zero, the embeddedness between the human body and the body of the parrot continues to fade; it fades, and fades, but doesn't fade to zero. This means that the parrot will still be a component of the speck of thought/awareness's Universal Feeling Body even after it itself has become unembedded with the nodes of feeling that are the parrot.

The situation is different in our mattress scenario. For, the two specks of thought/awareness that are situated in the two human bodies are each deeply embedded with nodes of feeling in both of the human bodies and the mattress. This is due to the long period of time that the two specks of thought/awareness have been in close spatial proximity to the two human bodies and the mattress. Furthermore, the human bodies, like the parrot, are originators of high intensity feelings. In this scenario, it would be a common occurrence for the speck of thought/awareness in one of the human bodies to become aware of the feelings that are located in the other human body, even when the two human bodies are significantly spatially-temporally separated.

It is very important for us to be clear what is going on here. A speck of thought/awareness in one of the human bodies is becoming directly aware of the nodes of feeling that are located in the other human body. Such direct awareness is possible because of three factors. Firstly, the other human body is contained within the Universal Feeling Body of the speck of thought/awareness. Secondly, spatial closeness between the speck of thought/awareness and this bit of its Universal Feeling Body. Of course, these two factors also apply in the pasty/parrot scenario. The third factor, which is what differentiates the mattress scenario, is the deep embeddedness that has been forged between each of the specks of thought/awareness and the two human bodies and the mattress, which enables awareness despite significant spatial-temporal separation. What is going on here is that a speck of thought/awareness is becoming aware of the feelings in various bits of its Universal Feeling Body in the same manner that it becomes aware of the feelings that are located in its animal body. A speck of thought/awareness is always deeply embedded with its animal body, but its embeddedness with the other bits of its Universal Feeling Body can range from extremely deeply embedded at one end of the spectrum, to unembedded at the other end of the spectrum. Spatial closeness in the present moment between a speck and a node always enables awareness of the feeling in the node. Whilst, the level of embeddedness between a speck and a node, the position on the spectrum, determines whether or not awareness persists during spatial-temporal separation.

Let us conclude. In our first scenario, the pasty, it is exceptionally unlikely that the speck of thought/awareness will ever become aware of any of the feelings that are the pasty. However, when we switched the pasty for a parrot, we saw that such awareness was almost inevitable if the nodes of feeling that are the parrot are high intensity feelings. This difference is due to the chasm in the level of feeling between the pasty and the parrot. In a similar vein, in our second scenario it is unlikely that either of the specks of thought/awareness will ever become aware of any of the feelings that are the mattress. There is a deep embeddedness here, but the mattress is only a collection of nodes of low-level feeling. In contrast, the speck of thought/awareness in one of the human bodies will regularly become aware of the feelings in the other human body due to the body having high intensity feelings. The crucial difference that distinguishes the parrot scenario from our second scenario is the level of embeddedness. In the parrot scenario, the speck of thought/awareness in the human body very quickly becomes unembedded with the parrot. In contrast, due to the deep embeddedness that exists in our second scenario, the specks of thought/awareness in the human bodies remain embedded with the other human body and the mattress during periods of significant spatial-temporal separation.

Universal unfolding to increasingly intense feelings

As the Universe unfolds it brings forth the possibility, and increasingly the reality, of increasingly intense feelings. This is the epic journey from inanimate (nodes of low-level feelings), to plant/fungi (nodes of medium-level feelings), to animal (nodes of high-level feelings). So, a tree has the potential to originate more intense feelings than a stone, whilst a bird has the potential to originate more intense feelings than a tree. Within each level of feeling, at different moments in time, in different locations in space, different intensities of feelings will exist. That is to say, at one moment in time, those parts of their observed Universe that humans call a bird, or a human, or a stone, or a tree, will contain more intense feelings than they do at another moment in time. And, if one beholds all of the plants, or all of the animals, that exist at a particular moment in time, then one will be beholding a vast array of different intensities and qualities of feeling.

To talk of conceptually moulded objects – a human, a bird, a tree, and a stone – in the context of Universal unfolding demands elucidation. For, conceptually moulded objects are the parts that constitute the observed Universe that is created by a speck of thought/awareness; whilst, the driving force of *Universal Unfoldment* are the feelings which constitute the unobserved Universe. So, that which is unfolding is not conceptually moulded parts; that which is unfolding is the borderless objectless entity that is the Universal Feeling Body. The obvious question that raises itself is: How are parts related to feelings in the process of *Universal Unfoldment?*

That which is borderless and objectless – the Universal Feeling Body – goes through a process of *Universal Unfoldment,* a process which results, at different stages of its unfoldment, in the bringing forth of potentially observable arrangements of itself, patterns of movement, that can be sensed in a particular way, and which a speck of thought/awareness can potentially conceptually mould into particular types of parts. Did that last sentence make sense to you? To put it simply, there is a correspondence between the levels of feeling that exist in the Universal Feeling Body (and the level of feeling that exists in a particular portion of the Universal Feeling Body), and the parts that a speck of thought/awareness can potentially conceptually mould the Universal Feeling Body into, following a visual sensing.

As the Universal Feeling Body unfolds it brings forth more intense feelings in nodes of feeling. Another way of putting this is to say that the process of *Universal Unfoldment* brings forth arrangements of the Universe that are increasingly complex – this is the movement from inanimate, to plant/fungi, to animal. This increasing feeling complexity explains the correspondence between the Universal Feeling Body and the observed Universe of parts. For, when an animal visually senses the Universe it senses distinctions between low-level feelings, medium-level feelings, and high-level feelings, despite not being able to sense the feelings themselves. That is to say, an animal can visually sense that a 'stone' is a very different kind of entity to a 'tree', and can visually sense that these two entities are very different kinds of entities to a 'human' and a 'tiger'. These visually sensed distinctions are grounded in the different complexity of the segments of the Universe that are visually sensed. That is to say, the visually sensed distinctions are grounded in different types of movement pattern. And, it is these visually sensed distinctions that inform the process that is the conceptual moulding of that which is visually sensed into distinct parts.

Feelings are movements

The feelings of the Universal Feeling Body are distinctive movements within the Universal Feeling Body. Low-level feelings have distinctive movement patterns. Medium-level feelings have distinctive movement patterns. And, high-level feelings have distinctive movement patterns. Envision a kangaroo jumping, a cheetah running, an eagle flying, and the London Marathon. Compare these movements to a tree swaying in the wind, mung beans sprouting, flowers flowering, and a Venus flytrap trapping. And compare these movements to raindrops falling, stone eroding, waves crashing, a pendulum swinging, and a sandstorm blowing.

A visual sensing is always a sensing of movement, whether it is a movement pattern that is sensed, or, whether there is an appearance of non-movement that is undergirded and suffused with actual movement. The sensing of movement, or apparent non-movement, is an indirect sensing of the feeling that underpins the movement.

The appearance of movement and non-movement

Every feeling in the Universal Feeling Body is in a continuous state of movement. That is to say, the entire Universe, every segment of it, is in a continuous state of movement. Yet, when a speck of thought/awareness seeks to make sense of the visual sensings that its visual sensory system presents it with, it is almost always presented with a mixture of that which moves in particular patterns, and that which appears not to move. Why is this? How can it be that what is continuously moving can appear not to move?

The answer to this question is obvious. Whether a particular segment of the Universe appears to be moving, and how it appears to be moving, or whether it appears to be not moving, is dependent on the structured nature of a particular visual sensing. In other words, where one visual sensory system senses non-movement, another visual sensory system will sense movement.

There is no other way of making sense of the apparent non-movement of that which is moving. If one becomes aware of apparent non-movement this is because one's visual sense has imposed order, a particular type of order, on that which is moving. In other words, one's visual sensings are coarse-grained extrapolators of the movements of the Universal Feeling Body.

The movement pattern of life

The segments of the Universe that are living have a distinctive movement pattern. They pull that which is not themselves into themselves, and they then expel that which they do not wish to appropriate into themselves out of themselves. This is a very different movement pattern from any of the movement patterns that existed prior to the bringing into existence of life in the Universe.

The movement pattern of life is a good example of the apparent non-movement of that which is moving, and also of the distinction between the movement patterns that are sensed and deeper more fine-grained movements which exist within these movements. For, when one's visual sense senses that segment of the Universe that one conceptually moulds as a 'tree', what will be visually sensed is either a movement pattern of an entity that is swaying in the wind, or an entity that is not moving. So, what is visually sensed is either the movement pattern of 'tree swaying' or 'non-movement'; yet, this segment of the Universe always contains the movement pattern that is 'metabolism'. That is to say, this segment of the Universe is the movement pattern of life.

The continuous two-way causation between feelings and movements

Every movement in the Universal Feeling Body entails, causes, a change in feeling. And, almost all of the movements in the Universal Feeling Body are caused by states of feeling. So, we have a continuous two-way causation between feelings and movements.

Feelings cause movements, and these movements cause changes in feeling, and these new feelings cause movements. The Universal Feeling Body unfolds. The Universe evolves.

The direct and indirect movements of a speck of thought/awareness

A tiny proportion of the movements in the Universal Feeling Body are not one hundred per cent caused by feelings. These are the movements that are initiated by specks of thought/awareness, either directly or indirectly.

Direct movements are the movements of an animal body which are instigated, brought into being, by the speck of thought/awareness that intermittently emerges in that animal body.

Indirect movements are any other movements that are initiated by a speck of thought/awareness. Indirect movements are many and varied: the flight of the football that has been kicked into the sky; the falling to the ground of the footballer that has been intentionally tripped; the movement of lead and dog as the dog's owner pulls the lead; the rolling of the stone that has been set on a journey down a hill; the movements of the ingredients as a cake is created; the flight of a space shuttle; the movement of the tennis ball that is in the mouth of a running dog; the orbit of a satellite; the movements of cars along roads, and trains along tracks; and, the movements of the robots that have been brought into existence by specks of thought/awareness.

The evolution of the visual sense to meet the needs of animals

Perhaps the notion of animals having visual sensory systems which are structured so as to indirectly sense different levels of feeling in the Universal Feeling Body seems a little fanciful to you. Or perhaps it sounds vague and is hard to make sense of. If so, it might help to envision what was happening in the Universe as animals evolved the ability to visually sense their surroundings. The evolution of this ability is grounded in an intricately developing interplay between that which is sensed and that which senses. Furthermore, this developing interplay is grounded in the needs of particular animals.

For instance, in order to survive animals need to be able to locate and acquire food; and, for many animals this entails evolving the ability to indirectly sense medium-level feelings. Through evolving the ability to visually sense plants/fruits/vegetables/fungi, animals effectively evolved the ability to sense that portion of the Universal Feeling Body that is the originator of medium-level feelings. If we envision our earliest human ancestors – we are talking prior to the invention of the bow and arrow, and the harpoon – these ancestors were not quick enough on their feet to be able to catch wild animals to eat for food. Their diet, their survival, was dependent on being able to visually sense plants, fruits, vegetables, and fungi. In other words, these humans had to be able to indirectly sense medium-level feelings. And their visual sense accomplished this by evolving so as to identify the movement patterns of medium-level feelings. When a human body visually senses the movement patterns of nodes of medium-level feeling in a particular way, this sensing enables its speck of thought/awareness to conceptually mould these patterns into the objects/parts that humans call plants, fruits, vegetables, and fungi.

In a similar vein, in order to survive animals need to be able to sense dangers/predators, and they also need to be able to locate potential mates. This means that animals needed to evolve the ability to visually sense the movements of nodes of high-level feeling. Some animals also need this ability to locate and acquire food. The visual sensing of the movements of nodes of high-level feeling is the structured sensing of movement patterns that a speck of thought/awareness in a human body might conceptually mould into parts such as: humans, dogs, cats, worms, tigers, sharks, rats, snakes, bees, elephants, spiders, fish, and seahorses.

So, the evolution of an animal's visual sense to meet its needs entails it sensing the movements of the Universal Feeling Body in a particular way. Structured visual sensings of different movement patterns provide the basis for a speck of thought/awareness to establish boundaries in what is sensed and thereby conceptually mould that which is visually sensed into distinct objects: parts. In this way, an observed Universe of parts comes into existence.

Esse est percipi and the Universal Moving Body

Berkeley realised a long time ago that for an object to be is for it to be perceived. This is fundamentally true. In the unobserved Universe there are no objects. For there to be a part in an observed Universe, it has to be perceived as a part. And, to be perceived as a part, is to be visually sensed in a particular way, and then to be taken by a speck of thought/awareness to be a part. Such sensing and taking is a moulding of the Universal Feeling Body into a distinct object.

Let us consider some examples. A part in my observed Universe is a block of vegan cheese. When I perceive the block of vegan cheese – when my human body visually senses this segment of the Universe and I then conceptually take it to be a part – it exists as a distinct object for me. If I put the block of vegan cheese into a refrigerator and close the door, you might want to assert that the block of vegan cheese still exists. If you were to assert such a thing, then you would be wrong. Esse est percipi. There is no mystery here. It is simply the case that the Universal Feeling Body – the unobserved Universe – is a boundaryless whole. For there to be an object within the whole, a boundary has to be brought into being by an act of perception.

The block of vegan cheese can be on a cheeseboard on a table that is in front of me. I perceive four entities as objects (block of vegan cheese, cheeseboard, table, my human body). I actively conceptually mould these segments of the Universe into distinct parts. When I close my eyes none of these four entities exists anymore as a distinct boundaried entity; for, my observed Universe of parts has gone out of existence, and all that exists is the unobserved Universe. One could loosely say that the block of vegan cheese has dissolved, dispersed, dissipated, into the Universal Feeling Body; but, it was in such a state even whilst it appeared as a distinct part in my observed Universe.

Let us consider a cat. You might think that the situation must be different with an animal, such as a cat. After all, is it really plausible to believe that the cats, dogs, humans, and so on, that are parts in my observed Universe, cease to exist when they are not perceived? You would be right to think that there is an important difference here. The situation with a cat is not fundamentally different from a block of vegan cheese. For a cat to exist as a distinct entity it needs to be perceived as such; in the absence of such a perception 'cat' movements are simply a miniscule component of the larger movement pattern that is the boundaryless Universal Feeling Body. *Indeed, the Universal Feeling Body could aptly also be called the Universal Moving Body.* When a cat is unperceived, its animal body is not a distinct boundaried part of the Universe. Yet, when the cat's speck of thought/awareness exists then an 'I' exists in the unobserved Universe, and the unobserved Universe is not affected by perception. A perceiver cannot bring a speck of thought/awareness into or out of existence through an act of perception. So, whilst a cat does not exist as a part when it is not perceived as a part, the speck of thought/awareness of a cat has a perceiver-independent existence. Like all specks of thought/awareness, the speck of thought/awareness of a cat has an intermittent existence; it is a currant which occasionally appears in the Universal bun; and, its body is its Universal Feeling Body.

You might currently be resistant to this picture. To say that a cat only exists as a distinct entity when it is perceived as such, but that its speck of thought/awareness has a perceiver-independent existence, is probably an unfamiliar way of thinking about your surroundings. For, I assume that your existence is probably currently wholly grounded in your observed Universe of parts. The truth of what has been said here only becomes blatantly apparent when one also has an existence in the unobserved Universe: the Universal Feeling Body. This book aims to take you on a gradual journey, which has as its destination a deep awareness of, and existence in, the Universal Feeling Body.

Visual sensing and the creation of conceptual mouldings

Let us get straight into the issue of the relationship between the parts that can be observed in an observed Universe – a block of vegan cheese, a cat, and so on – the visual sensory apparatus of an animal body, and the speck of thought/awareness that intermittently exists in an animal body.

The parts that are observed are segregated from their surroundings, boundaried, by a speck of thought/awareness. In other words, parts are conceptual creations; in the human realm, these segregations are given labels such as: 'cloud', 'lock', 'clock', 'cat', 'pillar', 'caterpillar', 'can', 'candle', 'bra', and 'candelabra'. We have already started to explore how such conceptual creations can either correspond to, or not correspond to, concrete differences in the Universal Feeling Body.

The visual sense of an animal – which incorporates its eyes and parts of its brain – senses the movements of the Universal Feeling Body in a particular way. Visual sensing itself is structured, and this structure is determined by the visual sense itself. In virtue of having very different visual senses, a human body will visually sense a very different observed Universe to a cat, a bee, a dolphin, a mouse, and a Tyrannosaurus Rex.

The structured nature of visual sensing is not itself sufficient to create parts. Parts are conceptual creations, conceptual mouldings, that only originate from a speck of thought/awareness. The structured nature of a particular visual sensing serves up a menu of possibilities for a speck of thought/awareness to conceptually carve up what has been sensed, and thereby to create an observed Universe of parts. So, to be perceived as a part, is to be visually sensed in a particular way, and then to be taken by a speck of thought/awareness to be a part. Such sensing and taking is a forging of the Universal Feeling Body into distinct objects.

So, there are two very distinct elements to visual perception: structured visual sensing, and conceptual moulding. Visual sensing itself could be thought of as a type of 'moulding', but it has no outputs, no objects, no parts. The existence of distinct entities, of parts, of boundaries, requires a conceptual moulding by a speck of thought/awareness.

Visual sensing on an alien planet

Envision that you are abducted by aliens and transported to their home planet. This planet, let us imagine, is an arrangement of the Universal Feeling Body that is totally unfamiliar to you. There are no movement patterns that can be visually sensed and conceptually moulded into parts such as: trees, birds, clouds, cats, and blocks of vegan cheese. There are just totally unfamiliar movements. When you first arrive on this planet your visual sensing of it will be structured so as to cause you to sense it in a particular way, but you won't encounter a world of parts! The appearance that you are encountered with will be a baffling undecipherable mess of intermingling stuff.

In order for there to be distinct parts, objects, within this initially baffling undecipherable mess, you – a speck of thought/awareness – need to get know this alien world. You need to impose order; you need to isolate pertinent movement patterns; you need to identify similarities within the initially undecipherable mess. Eventually boundaries will be established and labels will arise: a particular type of movement might be regularly spotted and labelled as a 'stfktdpod'. This label might refer to what is taken to be a particular type of alien life-form. Eventually your entire surroundings will be conceptually moulded in some way or other, and your observed Universe of parts is brought into being – a world that is wholly divided up into distinct parts. Yet, the baffling mess of intermingling stuff that you first encountered still exists, it has just been deciphered in a particular way, given your visual structuring combined with your strivings to make sense of the chaos.

Of course, what happens on the alien planet is what also occurs on the Earth. For, when animals on the Earth first developed the amazing ability to visually sense movements, their specks of thought/awareness were confronted with a baffling undecipherable mess of intermingling stuff. As time passed, as animals and their visual sensory systems evolved, these systems became increasingly specifically structured in order to latch on to movement patterns that are of importance for the survival of their animal bodies. And, each of these increasingly specifically structured visual sensory systems serve up a unique menu of possibilities for the specks of thought/awareness in diverse animal bodies to conceptually carve up the Universal Feeling Body.

Perception without awareness

Our considerations of the alien planet can help us to shed some light on the phenomenon of perception without awareness. For, visual sensing can clearly occur in the absence of a speck of thought/awareness. Such sensing is clearly a structuring of the Universe in a particular way. But the important question is: Can sensing without awareness bring into being an observed Universe? We are talking about a Universe that contains distinct parts such as 'cats', 'a block of vegan cheese', and 'stfktdpods'. The answer to this question is both 'no' and 'yes'.

Imagine that upon arrival on the alien planet your human body was visually sensing it but that you did not exist (there was no speck of thought/awareness in your human body). In this scenario there would be visual sensing, but no observed Universe of parts would come into being. There is just visual sensing of an intermingling undecipherable mess; there is no moulding of the Universe; there are no parts; there are no distinct objects. In this scenario, whilst there is visual sensing without awareness, there is no observed Universe of parts that is perceived. Esse est percipi. And nothing is perceived.

Now, imagine that you re-emerged, that a speck of thought/awareness re-emerged in the human body. Gradually, over time, as you analysed all of the visual sensings of your human body, as pertinent movement patterns were identified, the point would eventually come at which every component of every visual sensing would come to be conceptualised and labelled as something or other: 'stfktdpods', 'chullockses', 'splicdgcers', 'tpsolofods', and so on. Such concepts, such entities, such parts, will become embedded in the brain of your human body. This means that if, at a later time, your human body is visually sensing its surroundings in your absence – in the state of autopilot – then it can meaningfully be said to be not just visually sensing its surroundings, but also to be visually perceiving 'stfktdpods', 'chullockses', 'splicdgcers', and 'tpsolofods'.

 # The two types of embeddedness, and the question: Where is the location of origination of a feeling?

There are two types of embeddedness in the Universal Feeling Body; firstly, the embeddedness of a node of feeling with nodes of feeling; secondly, the embeddedness of a speck of thought/awareness with nodes of feeling. The first type of embeddedness arises due to the associations that are forged between nodes of feeling, as feelings feel each other, become associated with each other, and thereby fuse to form things. The instant radiation of feeling throughout things means that feelings are continuously being radiated into, and radiated out of, animal bodies. This means that whilst a speck of thought/awareness can know that a feeling exists, it might not know where it originated.

Let us turn to the second type of embeddedness, which involves a speck of thought/awareness becoming associated with feelings that exist in particular locations – in particular nodes of feeling – and thereby acquiring the potential to become aware of these feelings. These can be either feelings that exist within its close travelling companion – its animal body, or feelings that exist outside of this animal body in its wider Universal Feeling Body. In this type of embeddedness, a speck of thought/awareness becomes aware of the feeling that exists at the location at which it originates, whether this is in its close travelling companion, or elsewhere in its Universal Feeling Body.

What has just been said needs to be immediately clarified. A speck of thought/awareness becomes associated with nodes of feeling that exist at particular locations. This is clear enough. That which requires clarification is what it means to talk of the 'location of origination' of a feeling. For, the feeling in a particular location is not determined by the node of feeling at that location. It is true that when a node of feeling moves its feeling changes, but nodes of feeling get their movement and their feeling from feeling feelings that are not themselves. (If a speck of thought/awareness exists, it can also initiate movement in a node of feeling; these are the direct and indirect movements that we have already explored.) The feelings that are felt are the feelings that a node of feeling is associated with in the Universal Feeling Body. This is the co-radiation of feeling throughout things. This is co-feeling. This is things overlapping and underlaying each other, with one node of feeling participating in an immense plethora of things. Instant co-radiation of feeling throughout a thing provides a single feeling throughout a thing, a single feeling which is forever changing as every moment of time passes. A node of feeling participates in an immense plethora of things. Every node of feeling participates in a unique collection of things. This means that the feeling of a node is determined by the single feeling of all these things. A node differentially participates in all of its things — its feeling is more determined by some things than by other things. Every node of feeling has a unique feeling state. Unique feeling originates in every node of feeling, and this feeling radiates to, intermingles with, the nodes of feeling that the originating node is associated with. When one talks about the feeling that is originating, or that exists, in a particular location, a particular segment of the Universe, then one is talking about the process that has just been described.

The misery of the pet shop

If a speck of thought/awareness goes into a pet shop for the first time, then the close spatial proximity means that it becomes associated with the shop. This is the second type of embeddedness that we have just explored. In this situation, the entering of the pet shop, it is possible that the speck of thought/awareness might become overwhelmed by a feeling of misery, of despair. If this occurs, then the obvious explanation is that the speck of thought/awareness has become aware of the states of feeling that exist in the shops encaged inhabitants. It has reached outside of the illusory boundary that is the edges of its human body, and become aware of the high intensity feelings that exist in the animal bodies of the pet shop's encaged inhabitants. The feelings that are the encaged animal bodies have become a prominent component of the speck of thought/awareness's Universal Feeling Body.

Something else of importance is occurring here. For, the entering of the speck of thought/awareness into the pet shop is also, of course, the entering of its close travelling companion – its animal body – into the pet shop. The animal body and the pet shop will jointly participate in a plethora of things. This means that feelings will be radiated between the nodes of feeling of the animal body and the nodes of feeling of the pet shop. Particularly intense feelings, such as the feelings of misery and despair of the shop's encaged inhabitants – high intensity feelings – will dominate the things in which they participate. When the speck of thought/awareness enters the shop its animal body will be participating in an immense plethora of mediumly embedded things that incorporate these intense feelings of misery and despair. This means that the speck of thought/awareness might become aware of feelings in its own animal body that originated from the pet shop's encaged inhabitants. This is an awareness that is grounded in the first type of embeddedness that we recently explored.

The 3am awakening and the misattribution of feeling

A speck of thought/awareness emerges in a woman's body at 3am and instantly becomes aware of a feeling of excruciating unbearable pain that is accompanied by a sense of doom/despair. It is no surprise when she later finds out that it was at this exact time that her husband was shot and killed whilst he was on the other side of the world. The immense length of time that the speck that is her has been in exceptionally close spatial proximity to his human body has resulted in a very deep level of embeddedness, a deep potentiality to become aware of the feelings in his human body. Due to this it would be a common occurrence for her to become aware of the feelings that existed in his human body, although she would not normally realise that this was happening. Of course, her human body and his human body are also participants in an immense plethora of deeply embedded things, which means that in this scenario both of the types of embeddedness are in play. At 3am, feelings of extreme pain were radiated from his human body to her human body.

In this very extreme situation, the 3am awakening, the explanation for the terrible feelings that she became aware of, the dreadful cause of these feelings – the immense pain in the human body of her husband – was blatantly apparent. Typically the cause of this phenomenon is far from transparent; it is typically hidden. Due to the lack of knowledge of an obvious cause, the feelings that a speck becomes aware of are typically, and very understandably, misattributed as originating within its own animal body.

Nodes of feeling and things are saturated with memories

The unobserved Universe – the Universal Feeling Body – is a matrix of differentially interconnected feelings. Connections between feelings that are equally-embedded constitute things. Feelings are continuously originating in nodes, and such origination is occurring throughout the Universal Feeling Body. When feelings originate they instantly radiate throughout their things.

When some feelings feel each other they are attracted to each other, and increasingly become each other. When some feelings feel each other they are repulsed by each other, and go through a gradual divorce. Nodes of feeling, and the things that are forged by collections of nodes of feeling, contain memories of their previous feeling attractions and feeling repulsions. That is to say, they have feeling memories. More than this, nodes of feeling and things are saturated with feeling memories.

Envision a particular node of feeling that exists in the present moment; this node has the story of its past, its history, etched within itself. Its feeling interactions, its various attractions and repulsions, have shaped and forged it into the node of feeling that exists in the present moment. You can also envision a part, and imagine how what one conceptually moulds as a part has been forged through feeling attractions and feeling repulsions. For, the feelings of a part are the feelings of things. It is easy to assert that feelings *are* the fabric of the Universe. However, what this really means is that feeling memories are the fabric of the Universe. Feelings feel each other, and these feeling attractions and repulsions get etched into their nodes.

When feelings move in the Universal Feeling Body, and when feelings radiate throughout their things in the Universal Feeling Body, feeling memories are moving and radiating through the Universal Feeling Body. These feeling memories become stored in things in accordance with the degree of embeddedness of the thing – deeply embedded things are much greater repositories of feeling memories than weakly embedded things. Furthermore, there is a strong connection between the storage of feeling memories in nodes of feeling and the intensity of the feeling. High intensity feelings make more of a mark, are stored more vibrantly, than less intense feelings. The more intense a feeling is, the more vibrantly it is stored.

The storage of feeling memories and the creation of 'shining beacons'

The storage of feeling memories in the Universal Feeling Body means that if a particular location exists which generates high intensity feelings in a large number of animal bodies, then this location will become radiantly and increasingly imbued with this feeling. Such places gradually become increasingly intense 'shining beacons', lighthouses of feeling, within the Universal Feeling Body. The feelings in these 'shining beacons' will have a specific quality, as well as a specific intensity. One can easily envision high intensity feelings of a particular quality being widely, consistently, and continuously, generated in specific locations.

Envision locations such as places of worship and pilgrimage, football stadiums, libraries, nightclubs, prisons, haunted houses, abattoirs, and fairgrounds. The feelings generated in these particular places, by the plethora of animal bodies that spend time there, are likely to be of a similar quality. These feelings will become increasingly reinforced and embedded and will become the hallmark of the place. The euphoria of the nightclub, the despair of the prison, the joy of the fairground, the intellectual stillness of the library, the tribal excitement of the football stadium, the misery of the abattoir, the bliss of the place of worship, and the state of feeling scared/terrified at the haunted house.

The hallmark of a segment of the Universe is the quality and intensity of the feeling states that exist in this portion of the Universal Feeling Body.

Shining beacons of feeling

When one beholds the Universal Feeling Body as a whole one will be aware that certain bits of it stand out, protrude, as if they were torches illuminating a vast sea of darkness. These shining beacons are epicentres of deeply embedded feelings of a particular quality.

The brightest shining beacons, those that protrude the most, those that are the most radiant, are formed by deeply embedded high intensity feelings. Such feelings can be generated by any segment of the Universe that intermittently brings into existence a speck of thought/awareness. That is to say, such feelings can be generated by any animal body. So, one can surely appreciate that locations such as abattoirs, vivisection centres, and war zones, will be segments of the Universe that are epicentres, shining beacons, of highly embedded feelings of suffering, desperation, and despair. In contrast, places such as meditation centres and places of worship will be epicentres, shining beacons, of more wholesome feelings.

Shining beacons need not be formed by high intensity feelings. They can be formed by feelings of any intensity, if such feelings are sufficiently deeply embedded with each other. Two factors combine so as to bolster radiance – increasing embeddedness and increasing intensity – if the combination of these two factors is above a certain threshold, then the radiance of the location will be sufficient to create a shining beacon.

 # No feeling is an island; networks of feelings

Every feeling in the Universal Feeling Body is determined by that which it is associated with. 'No feeling is an island' is an appropriate phrase. The Universal Feeling Body is a matrix of differentially embedded feeling connections. Sites of deeply embedded feeling of a particular quality and sufficient intensity are shining beacons within this matrix. When a new feeling arises, it does not arise in a vacuum. A new feeling is a transmutation of a feeling in a node of feeling. A new feeling arises within networks of things. That is to say, it arises within networks of interconnected feeling nodes. A 'thing' is a network of nodes, each of which originates one of the three levels of feeling. When a feeling is originated in a node it is instantly radiated throughout its things. Some networks of feelings are small. Some networks of feelings are enormous. That which is in one network, will be in other networks; for, every feeling is differentially embedded with other feelings in the Universal Feeling Body. This means that there are networks of networks; networks that spatially overlap and underlay each other.

A new feeling changes the feeling of all of the feelings in a thing. A network of feelings is a network of associations/embeddedness; it is those feelings in the Universal Feeling Body that are equally-associated with each other. To say that a new feeling emerges within things, is to say that this feeling is felt throughout these things. Every feeling in a thing modifies the feeling state of every feeling in a thing; for, this is what it is to be a thing. Whilst feelings originate in particular locations, they are felt throughout the things in which they participate.

All of the parts that constitute one's observed Universe are constituted out of things. A thing does not have a discrete location, in the way that the parts of an observed Universe do. However, all of the constituents of a thing are inevitably located somewhere. In conceptually moulding one's structured visual sensings into distinct parts, creating boundaries, one is extrapolating from overlapping networks of things.

The concepts of the observed Universe and the baby in the womb

The parts that one conceptually moulds are, fundamentally, things. The parts that are moulded are participants in networks of feelings. When we focus on our observed Universe our attempt to describe the world that appears is grounded in concepts. We can talk of: a chair, a pencil, a cloud, a planet, a baby in a womb, an adult human, a tree, a leaf, a root, a beetroot, a corpse, a copse, a square, and a squirrel.

We might assert that when a baby is in its mother's womb, that its feelings are determined by the feelings that are its mother's body. Now, of course, this is correct. The baby, and its mother's womb, and its mother, are all components of particular things that are engaged in a continuous process of co-feeling. However, when we describe the situation using human concepts we are getting a very partial view of what is going on. If we switch from the observed Universe of parts, and focus on the unobserved Universe of things, then we can appreciate that the baby in the womb is a collection of nodes of high-level feeling that are participants in things. Furthermore, we can appreciate that the nodes of feeling in the baby both affect, and are determined by, these entire networks.

High intensity feelings enliven and amplify each other

It will be fruitful for us to consider what happens when a group, and in particular a large group, of animal bodies gather in a particular location. Animal bodies are collections of nodes of the top category of feeling – high-level feeling – and therefore are the entities that originate the most intense feelings that exist in the Universe. We have already considered the existence of shining beacons of feeling, and we saw that the brightest shining beacons are those that are created by high intensity feelings. One factor in play in the creation of shining beacons is the effect that two high intensity feelings have on each other. *High intensity feelings are enlivened and amplified when in the presence of other high intensity feelings.* The more of such feelings that exist in a particular location, the more pronounced that this effect will be.

If one is in a massive crowd of animal bodies – at a rock concert, on a demonstration, in a packed nightclub, crammed liked sardines into a train carriage, surrounded by a family of sardines in the ocean, at a religious festival, in a factory farm, or in the middle of a stampede, then the feelings of one's human body will be amplified and enlivened by the presence of the crowd. This effect will continue for some time after the crowd has dispersed. Amplification and enlivenment is inevitable in these circumstances, but it says nothing about the quality of the feelings that exist. One's human body could be amplified and enlivened in a euphoric way whilst in a packed nightclub. One's human body could be amplified and enlivened in a mournful way whilst at a funeral that is attended by thousands of human bodies.

Feeling memory/recognition/familiarity

The amplification and enlivenment of high intensity feelings that occurs in a crowd of animal bodies is an exacerbation of the forging of links of association that can occur between any two bits of the Universal Feeling

Body. It is the epitome of feelings feeling feelings: high intensity feelings are jointly sharing the depths of themselves.

Throughout the Universal Feeling Body, increasing spatial closeness, and a longer duration of time spent at spatial closeness, results in deepening embeddedness. The forging of these deepening bonds entails increasing feeling memory/recognition/familiarity.

That which has been felt becomes familiar; memories are etched.
That which has been felt is recognised when re-encountered.

Changing bonds of embeddedness and feeling amplification

There is an intricate interplay between the forging of links of spatial association and the forging of links of temporal association within the Universal Feeling Body. The bonds forged by closer spatial proximity are bolstered the longer the period of time that this spatial proximity exists. And the bonds that are forged by closer spatial proximity will fade over time if this spatial proximity increases.

If the bond of embeddedness between two nodes is fragile/weak then it will rapidly fade; whereas, if the bond of embeddedness between two nodes is robust/strong then it will fade very gradually. Bonds formed at a farther spatial proximity can be more robust than those formed at a closer spatial proximity. This occurs when the duration of time for which the proximity exists is sufficiently greater to outweigh the farther spatial proximity.

When considering the ever-changing nature of these bonds, the golden rule to keep in mind is: *a feeling state amplifies and enlivens that which feels as intensely as itself, and that which feels less intensely than itself.* So, for example, a low-level feeling will not amplify and enliven a medium-level feeling, but a medium-level feeling will amplify and enliven a low-level feeling.

 # Two associated nodes have a single bond; two associated parts have an immense plethora of bonds

It will be fruitful to say a little more about bonds of embeddedness. The Universal Feeling Body is constituted out of nodes of feeling. Take any two nodes of feeling and these two nodes can have, at the most, one bond of embeddedness that connects them. There cannot be two bonds connecting the same two nodes. The issue of whether every node of feeling in the Universal Feeling Body has a bond to every other node of feeling in the Universal Feeling Body is an issue that we will return to in due course.

Our current concern is simply to appreciate that there can only be one bond of embeddedness between two nodes of feeling. The nature of this bond varies greatly. The bond can be so weak that the two nodes barely feel each other; in this case, the two nodes are almost not connected. At the other extreme, the bond can be so strong, so deep, that the two nodes effectively share all of their feeling with each other. In this case, the two nodes almost become each other. There are an immense plethora of gradations between these two extremes.

Now, when we are talking about the observed Universe, we are talking about conceptually moulded parts. The situation is different from this perspective. We are not now going to be talking about a single bond of embeddedness. We are going to be saying that there are an immense plethora of bonds of embeddedness that connect a human body to the tree that it is standing underneath. There are an immense plethora of bonds because the two parts jointly participate in an immense plethora of things.

The plethora of gradations of feeling associations

One can try to envision the immense plethora of gradations of feeling associations that exist within the Universal Feeling Body. We have explored some of the associations that are forged between the feelings that exist in two human bodies, and the associations that are forged between the feelings that exist in a particular human body and the feelings that exist in non-human bits of the Universal Feeling Body. Of course, the changing associations, the coalescence, the forging and fusing of feelings, the unforging and unfusing of feelings, and the coming into being of increasing familiarity, occurs throughout the Universal Feeling Body.

As every moment of time passes, the things that exist in the segment of the Universe that can be moulded as a 'body part' of an 'animal body' will be forging increasing bonds of feeling with some nodes of feeling in the Universal Feeling Body, whilst simultaneously becoming less embedded with some other nodes of feeling in the Universal Feeling Body. So, these things will simultaneously be acquiring feelings and loosing feelings. Every movement that a body part makes – from the beating of a heart, to the blinking of an eyelid, to the raising of a finger – entails changes in spatial position within the Universal Feeling Body. A change in spatial position inevitably entails the passage of time. Every movement that a body part makes, and any movement in the entire Universal Feeling Body, initiates a cascade of changing spatial-temporal associations between nodes of feeling, as feelings both move and radiate throughout things. Some feeling associations are strengthened, whilst others are inevitably weakened, and in this way a plethora of new things are forged. There is no state of 'no-change'. Feeling associations are continuously changing, even if only by a miniscule amount. The result of this is the plethora of gradations of feeling associations.

A body within the body

A speck of thought/awareness has the Universal Feeling Body as its body. A speck of thought/awareness has its strongest links of association, both spatial and temporal, with the animal body which it intermittently emerges within. One can picture the movement of the body parts of an animal within the Universal Feeling Body as one comes to appreciate the forever changing links of feeling association that are being forged in the things that these body parts participate in. Things that whilst existing in an animal body, are not constrained by the boundaries of that body. For, the boundary of an animal body is an arbitrary delineation that is created/imposed by a particular perceiver. So, whilst an animal body that is taken to be a part in an observed Universe can map onto a collection of nodes of origination of high-level feelings in the unobserved Universe, the things that these nodes participate in typically extend way beyond the boundaries of the animal body. The feeling connections that constitute a thing are not constrained by the moulded Universe of parts – parts such as a human body.

A body within the body. A human head, torso, arms, and legs, moving through the Universal Feeling Body in a similar way to the way that blood moves/flows through a human body. A continuous movement. A continuous flow. Yet, a process that has no boundaries.

Moulded parts are collections of feeling nodes and are components of things

It will be fruitful for us to draw some threads together from our recent explorations into various aspects of the Universal Feeling Body. We have considered how high intensity feelings amplify and enliven each other. In other words, when a crowd of animal bodies is in a particular segment of the Universe, and particularly when the setting of their meeting is emotionally charged in some way – whether a football match, a funeral, or an abattoir – then the animal bodies amplify and enliven each other.

What is happening here can be made more intelligible if one envisions what is going on in the Universal Feeling Body. For, as we reminded ourselves in the previous section, the boundary of an animal body is an arbitrary delineation that is carved by a perceiver. What a speck of thought/awareness might visually perceive as an animal body in their observed Universe, is, in the Universal Feeling Body, a collection of nodes of origination of high-level feeling. However, this collection of feeling nodes does not necessarily match the moulded boundary of an animal body that is created by a perceiver. For, a plethora of diverse perceivers can each carve up a segment of the Universe in different ways. This is, for sure, a little mind-boggling; it is something that we will flesh out in our future explorations into the Universal Feeling Body.

Collections of feeling nodes are unaffected by observation, but they can be moulded by perceivers into diverse boundaried entities/objects/parts. The nodes of feeling themselves participate in an immense plethora of things; so, the moulded parts that a perceiver perceives are forged out of, and are components of, these things.

The leaching of feelings from animal bodies

To talk of an animal body as an originator of high-level feelings, is to say that this segment of the Universe is a collection of nodes of high-level feelings which, through their participation in an immense plethora of things, are radiating high-level feelings, including high intensity feelings, throughout the things in which the nodes participate. In terms of the observed Universe, you can envision an animal body as a source from which high-level feelings leach, percolate, stream, flow, into the surrounding Universe.

From this perspective, it is surely much easier to appreciate how high intensity feelings come to amplify and enliven each other. For, these high intensity feelings are leaching out of each of the animal bodies that is in a crowd, and flowing through the other animal bodies in the crowd, due to these bodies jointly participating in an immense plethora of things. The longer that the crowd exists, and the more tightly packed together that it is, the more profound that this phenomenon will be; for, the feelings will be leaching and diffusing within increasingly deeply embedded things.

The differential visual sensing and conceptual moulding of nodes and modes

For the sake of clarity we need to delve a little deeper into some of the issues that we have just been exploring. So, the first point to make clear is that there is a fact of the matter concerning the nature and location of nodes of feeling in the Universal Feeling Body. Every bit of the Universal Feeling Body will have, at a specific location, a node of low-level feeling, or a node of medium-level feeling, or a node of high-level feeling.

The second point to make clear is that there is a cast-iron relationship between these different levels of nodes of feeling, and the three modes of the Universe. In other words, nodes of low-level feeling are inanimate segments of the Universe, nodes of medium-level feeling are segments of the Universe that are living without thought/awareness, and nodes of high-level feeling are segments of the Universe that are living with thought/awareness. There might seemingly be exceptions to this cast-iron relationship: where nodes of high-level feeling exist, but the capacity to generate a speck of thought/awareness has been lost. So, to avoid any possible confusion, it should be made explicit that the phrase 'living with thought/awareness' refers to living animal bodies whose speck of thought/awareness has an intermittent existence; the phrase refers to such animal bodies even when its speck does not exist. Following the vast majority of these episodes of non-existence the speck re-emerges.

The third point to make clear, which might seem very strange, given the first two points, is: esse est percipi. The act of perceiving a particular segment of the Universe – which is a particular movement pattern of nodes of feeling – brings into being perceived entities – parts – that are perceiver-dependent. For, the structured nature of visual sensing, which isolates a movement pattern within a movement pattern, combined with conceptual moulding, can lead to the same movement pattern of nodes of feeling in the unobserved Universe being perceived very differently.

Movement patterns in the observed Universe versus the unobservable 'one giant movement pattern'

It is very important to try and grasp that the unobserved Universe – the Universal Feeling Body – is one giant movement pattern, a pattern that is not affected by observation, and which is very different to the movement patterns that one visually perceives. The movement patterns that one perceives are the movements of the parts that one has conceptually moulded. And, these conceptual mouldings, in turn, are grounded in one's structured visual sensings of the one giant movement pattern.

The one giant movement pattern cannot be observed. The movement patterns that one's visual sense detects are extrapolations from the one giant movement pattern; and, the nature of these extrapolations are determined by the structure of one's visual sensory apparatus. The one giant movement pattern can, through differential visual sensing, be carved up into an almost infinite number of movement patterns. The movement patterns that are visually sensed are related to the movement that is occurring in the one giant movement pattern in this segment of the Universe; yet, very different movement patterns can simultaneously be detected, by different visual sensory systems, in this same segment of the Universe. Visual sensing isolates a movement pattern within the movement pattern.

The 'two-headed kangaroo'

We need to explore further the differential visual sensing and conceptual moulding of nodes and modes. *Visual perception has two components: visual sensing which is carried out by an animal body, and conceptual moulding which is carried out by a speck of thought/awareness.* In this section, we will be focusing on the second stage of visual perception: conceptual moulding.

As we are focusing here on the second stage of visual perception, we are exploring the attempt of a speck of thought/awareness to make sense of what has been visually sensed. Let us consider a particular segment of the Universe that is visually sensed. Let us assume that this segment of the Universe contains nodes of high-level feeling = is the mode of living with thought/awareness. This bit of the Universal Feeling Body thus has distinctive movement patterns – both the movement pattern of life, and the movement pattern of an animal.

When a speck of thought/awareness strives to make sense of what has been visually sensed it latches on to the movement patterns that have been sensed. In particular, it latches on to how segments of the Universe appear to be either moving, or not moving, in relation to other segments. If the movement pattern that is sensed is seemingly a distinct singular entity, when it is contrasted to surrounding segments – an entity that is moving through its surroundings in a particular way, moving in a certain way against the backdrop of its surroundings – then a speck of thought/awareness is likely to delineate this movement as an entity, as a distinct object: a part. Indeed, this is precisely how a speck of thought/awareness comes to conceptualise the animal body that it intermittently emerges within as a distinct boundaried entity: a part.

The segment of the Universe that we are considering here, a segment that contains nodes of high-level feeling, is a segment that a speck of thought/awareness in a human body conceptually moulds and labels as:

a 'two-headed kangaroo'. This part has been conceptually moulded out of the movement patterns that have been visually sensed. The 'two-headed kangaroo' is a part in this speck of thought/awareness's observed Universe.

Let us now consider a speck of thought/awareness in another human body that was presented with the same visual sensing – exactly the same movement pattern. This speck could conceptually mould this movement pattern into two distinct entities. This means that the same segment of the Universe has, simultaneously, been conceptually carved up into one part and into two parts. This difference in conceptual moulding arises due to this second speck of thought/awareness having the belief that one of the heads is a head of a joey that is in its mother's marsupial pouch.

Given that a joey stays in the marsupial pouch for over half a year, if one were sensing the movements of this segment of the Universe for months, one would have no compelling reason to suspect that there were two animals here, rather than one; unless, that is, one had prior knowledge concerning the mating and upbringing behaviour of kangaroos.

So, in our scenario we have a particular segment of the Universe that contains a collection of nodes of high-level feeling = is the mode of living with thought/awareness. Two human bodies are visually sensing this exact same segment in an identical manner, and yet one speck of thought/awareness conceptually carves it up into one part, whilst the other conceptually carves it up into two parts. It is not obviously the case that one of these specks is correct and the other is mistaken. For, the segment of the Universe in question could have been a kangaroo with two heads, or it could have been a joey in the marsupial pouch of its mother. If the two specks were debating what they had visually perceived, they would not be able to reach a conclusion as to who was right and who was wrong – it could have been a 'two-headed kangaroo', or it could have been a 'joey in the marsupial pouch of its mother'.

Given that all of the parts in an observed Universe are created by a particular speck of thought/awareness, the whole notion of being able to be 'correct' or 'mistaken' about this issue might seem to be misplaced. The subject of the debate between our two specks is really whether the movement pattern that has been visually sensed could potentially split into two distinct and spatially separated movement patterns. This is a question which has a definite singular answer. Such judgements are actually at the core of the processes that are continuously at work as a speck of thought/awareness seeks to make sense of the movement patterns that it is presented with. So, the debate between our two specks, is, effectively, the 'internal debate' that goes on within a speck of thought/awareness as it tries its best to make sense of the movement patterns that it is continuously bombarded with.

Is it a kangaroo, a flock of birds, or the Solar System?

We can now continue our exploration of the differential visual sensing and conceptual moulding of nodes and modes by focusing on the first stage of visual perception: visual sensing. Visual sensing is a structured activity that is structured by the visual sensory system. If we start with the human visual sensory system we can appreciate that it is structured in such a way that when it senses particular movement patterns, these movement patterns can possibly be conceptually moulded by a speck of thought/awareness into parts such as 'kangaroos' and 'two-headed kangaroos'. More than this, my visual sensory system is structured so as to enable me to conceptually mould parts such as 'tables', 'trees', 'candles', 'pineapples', 'tigers', 'clouds', 'mushrooms', and 'stars'.

The human visual sensory system is unique to human bodies. There are a plethora of diverse and very different visual sensory systems on the Earth. Each of these systems provides a different structure, a different way of extrapolating movement patterns from the one giant movement pattern. This means that these very different structures provide very different possibilities and opportunities for specks of thought/awareness to conceptually mould their surroundings. In turn, this means that some specks of thought/awareness cannot possibly conceptually mould their surroundings into anything that even remotely resembles a 'kangaroo' or a 'two-headed kangaroo'.

The nodes and mode in the segment of the Universe that a human perceives a 'two-headed kangaroo' could be visually sensed in a much more fine-grained way. So, where the visual sensory system of a human senses 'large' movements: an entity the size of a kangaroo leaping up in to the air, and bounding through its surroundings, a more visually fine-grained sensory system could be structured so as to sense a plethora of much smaller much more refined movement patterns. In this situation, what exactly would be visually sensed?

Perhaps one can get a handle on what might be sensed as follows: *the visual sensory system of a human senses 'a single bounding movement', but more fine-grained visual sensory systems might sense the movement pattern that is 'a flock of birds repeatedly diving and then rising up through the sky'.* In other words, the movements of the nodes and the mode that exists in this segment of the Universe can be perceived at different levels of granularity. If a speck of thought/awareness is confronted with a movement pattern that has been sensed as a 'flock of birds' diving and rising, then it is likely to conceptually mould this segment of the Universe into a plethora of different parts. Whereas, the speck of thought/awareness in a human, which is presented with a 'single bounding movement', will conceptually mould one part – a 'two-headed kangaroo', or two parts – a 'joey' and a 'female adult kangaroo'.

We should explore a little what it means for a 'flock of birds' to be visually sensed in the segment of the Universe that the speck of thought/awareness in a human conceptually moulds as a kangaroo. Of course, 'birds' aren't visually sensed; for, a 'bird' is a conceptual moulding made by a speck of thought/awareness. We are here using the phrase 'flock of birds' to point towards what has been visually sensed in this segment of the Universe prior to a conceptual moulding. What is visually sensed is a tightly bound collection of tiny entities that are moving in unison – in lockstep – with each other. The movement pattern that is visually sensed is not one large movement (a pattern that could possibly be conceptually moulded into a kangaroo); what is visually sensed is a multitude of tiny entities that, as a collective, move in roughly the same way as the one large 'bounding' movement pattern that is sensed by humans.

Does this all sound a bit bonkers to you? If so, then it might help to reflect on your conceptual moulding in your observed Universe that is an actual flock of birds flying through the sky in lockstep – diving and rising in formation. When you visually sense this segment of the Universe, you, no doubt, conceptualise it as lots of parts: lots of 'birds'. Whereas, if an alien observer who had no concept of a 'bird' visually sensed this movement pattern, then it is quite easy to appreciate how it could conceptually mould it into a single part. For you, there are lots of 'birds'; for the alien observer there is but one part – a part that it might conceptually mould and label as a 'kangaroo'. But this is not just about conceptual moulding; the alien observer also has a different structured visual sensing of this segment of the Universe. Perhaps, in this scenario, the alien observer is a coarse-grained sensor (kangaroo), and you are the fine-grained sensor (flock of birds). Where it senses 'one', you sense 'many'.

There is a need here to be clear. So, to repeat, there is a fact of the matter concerning the state of the Universal Feeling Body in the segment of the Universe that we are considering. That is to say, there is a fact of the matter concerning the number and feeling level of nodes of feeling that exist in this particular segment; a fact of the matter concerning the existence of specks of thought/awareness in this segment of the Universe; and, a fact of the matter concerning the movements of the one giant movement pattern. What is perceiver-dependent is the granularity of the movement patterns that are visually sensed, patterns which provide a particular range of possibilities for conceptual moulding of that which has been visually sensed.

There is an intimate connection between the granularity of the movement patterns that are visually sensed and the appearance of non-movement in that which is moving. A more fine-grained sensing will sense more movement and less non-movement. A more coarse-grained sensing will sense less movement and more non-movement.

Let us put more flesh on the bones of our scenario. The segment of the Universe that we have been considering could be visually perceived as a 'kangaroo' (or a 'two-headed kangaroo') or it could be visually perceived as a 'flock of birds'; yet, there is, in the unobserved Universe, just one reality concerning the existence of specks of thought/awareness. This segment of the Universe contains no specks of thought/awareness, one speck of thought/awareness, or a particular number of specks of thought/awareness greater than one. Furthermore, this segment of the Universe, in the unobserved Universe, contains a plethora of nodes of high-level feeling that are moving in a particular way. Yet, this feeling is unobservable, and this movement can only be observed in a structured way. A visual sensing is a structured extrapolation of the one giant movement pattern. And, a multitude of different extrapolations of this segment of the Universe are possible.

The nodes and mode in a particular segment of the Universe – that segment in which a human perceives a 'two-headed kangaroo' and a more fine-grained perceiver perceives a 'flock of birds' – could be visually sensed in a much more coarse-grained way. Such a sensing entails 'zoning out' and sensing much broader movement patterns. What a human visually senses as a 'single bounding movement', is, in such a coarse-grained sensing, far too tiny to be sensed. The 'single bounding movement' effectively vanishes into its surroundings. From the coarse-grained perspective, the 'single bounding movement' is so miniscule that it is not identifiable as a movement pattern in its own right. Indeed, it has become non-movement.

Perhaps one can get a handle on what might be sensed as follows: *the visual sensory system of a human senses 'a single bounding movement', but a more coarse-grained visual sensory system senses the movement pattern that is 'our Solar System'.* From this coarse-grained perspective, the movement patterns of 'humans', 'kangaroos', 'trees', and 'cars', are all far too small to be noticed. One can imagine that a coarse-grained sensing is not able to sense any movement patterns on the Earth. Yet, when the sensory apparatus gazes away from the Earth it is able to behold a movement pattern – the movement of the Moon around the Earth, and the movements of the planets in our Solar System as they circle the Sun. Such movements are large enough to be able to be sensed as a movement pattern.

Medium-grained sensing

Beholding only movement patterns that are as large as the movements of celestial bodies is an extreme case of coarse-grained visual sensing. Envisioning such a possibility is useful. Yet, as we have already explored, the visual sensory systems that have evolved on the Earth have evolved so as to meet the needs of their animal bodies. The survival of animal bodies is not aided by being only able to sense movement patterns as big as the movements of the celestial bodies! Survival requires meeting needs such as detecting the movement patterns that are 'predators', 'dangers', 'mates', and 'food'. This means that the visual sensory systems that have evolved on the Earth have evolved to sense movements such as: 'flames flickering', 'tiger running', 'spider approaching', 'shark swimming', 'plant swaying', and 'eagle swooping'.

Perceiving movement patterns in this way, what we can call a 'medium-grained' way, entails sensing apparent non-movement in large swathes of the Universe; for, the entire Universe is moving in a more fine-grained way than animals can visually detect. So, one can visually perceive entities that appear not to be moving: an 'apple', a 'coconut', a 'tree', and a 'stone'. Yet, these segments of the Universe would be movement patterns to a more fine-grained visual sensing.

We can fruitfully use the term 'medium-grained sensing' to refer to all of the visual sensory systems that have evolved on the Earth. Within the realm of 'medium-grained sensing' there is a range of granularity, with some visual sensory systems sensing movement where others sense non-movement. On the Earth there is no 'ultra-fine-grained' sensing, which would entail animals evolving visual sensory systems that sensed the movement patterns of atoms. On the Earth there is no 'coarse-grained' sensing, which would entail only sensing movement patterns as big as the movements of the celestial bodies.

The Stages of Universal Unfoldment

The arrangements of the Universal Feeling Body that generate – bring into being – specks of thought/awareness are collections of nodes of high-level feeling. Given this correlation, it should be clearly understood that a speck does not create high-level feeling. To the contrary, it is some of the movement patterns of nodes of high-level feeling that generate specks of thought/awareness in the third stage of Universal Unfoldment. As the Universe unfolds it goes through various stages. As the *Stages of Universal Unfoldment* progress from A) non living, to B) living without thought/awareness, to C) living with thought/awareness, the intensity of feeling that exists automatically increases. For, it is the striving for more intense feeling that is the driving force behind Universal Unfoldment. Such striving brings into existence more complex movement patterns, patterns which feel more intensely, which means that each of the *Stages of Universal Unfoldment* has its own characteristic movement patterns. *The Universal Feeling Body feels more intensely as it evolves and unfolds.*

The three distinct *Stages of Universal Unfoldment* directly correspond to the coming into existence of the three different levels of feeling. In Stage A) of Universal Unfoldment only nodes of low-level feeling exist. In Stage B) nodes of medium-level feeling are brought forth into existence. In Stage C) nodes of high-level feeling are brought forth into existence. This means that the coming into existence of more intense feelings is an indication that the *Stages of Universal Unfoldment* are progressing.

The disgusting conception

The Universal Feeling Body likes to feel more intensely. This is not surprising; for, what could be more precious and valuable than being able to feel, and to be able to feel more and more intensely! How disgusting it is to try and imagine a possible Universe that is devoid of feeling – comprised wholly of unfeeling entities; a mere mechanism that is comprised of robotic unfeeling actions/movements. Indeed, it is hard to imagine anything that could possibly be more grotesque than such a miserable abomination.

The Stages of Universal Unfoldment – the two standpoints

The *Stages of Universal Unfoldment* have one direction, but this can be approached from two standpoints. The first standpoint is the movement towards the origination of increasingly intense feeling. Every thing that exists, every feeling that exists, is striving to transform itself into more intense feeling, whenever, and wherever, it possibly can. It is this striving that gives the impetus to Universal Unfoldment, both in terms of the movement from one stage to another stage in the three *Stages of Universal Unfoldment,* and in terms of the movements of the Universal Feeling Body within each stage. One encounters this process of directed striving unfoldment whenever one beholds the Universal Feeling Body. The movements towards the origination of increasingly intense feeling are typically gradual, with the exceptions being the two mini-chasms; for, when these chasms open up in the Universal Feeling Body there is a stark jump in the feeling intensity that exists.

The second standpoint from which one can approach the *Stages of Universal Unfoldment* becomes crystal clear when we switch from the unobserved Universe to the observed Universe. This is the movement from the non-living, to living without thought/awareness, to living with thought/awareness. *In other words, the transformation of nodes of feeling and things as they evolve new movement patterns that feel more intensely is the journey that is the movement towards life, followed by the movement towards more complex life-forms.* The two enormous jumps in movement pattern complexity are the bringing forth of life and the bringing forth of specks of thought/awareness.

Awareness participates in increasingly complex thought

The movement towards complexity pervades the *Stages of Universal Unfoldment*. This means that the bringing into being of the first speck of thought/awareness is followed by the movement towards increasingly complex specks of thought/awareness. Such movement is, effectively, the movement towards increasingly complex thought. For, awareness cannot get more complex – it simply either exists or it does not exist. It is not a phenomenon that can vary in complexity! *So, to talk of specks of thought/awareness getting more complex, is to say that awareness is participating in increasingly complex thought.*

The purpose of specks of thought/awareness within the Stages of Universal Unfoldment

An obvious question that we need to address is: Why are the *Stages of Universal Unfoldment* directed towards the bringing forth of specks of thought/awareness? We also need to ask the question: Why is there a movement towards increasingly complex specks of thought/awareness? Or, similarly: What is the purpose of specks of thought/awareness? The answer is obvious: *the purpose of a speck of thought/awareness is to steer and guide its animal body so as to enable this body to flourish, to actualise its potential, to utilise its abilities/skills/aptitudes. And, the more complex that a speck of thought/awareness is, the more able it is to fulfil this mission.*

This answer to our questions is grounded in my observed Universe of parts (animal bodies). When we switch our standpoint to the unobserved Universe then we are able to give another equally valid answer to our questions: *the purpose of a speck of thought/awareness is to steer and guide things so as to enable them to transform themselves into increasingly intense feelings of attraction. And, the more complex that a speck of thought/awareness is, the more able it is to fulfil this mission.*

A speck of thought/awareness has a foot in both worlds – the observed Universe and the unobserved Universe. When one takes a step back and beholds the entire process of the *Stages of Universal Unfoldment,* then one can see that the striving of feelings to feel more intensely has resulted in them coming into various movement patterns, and that the outcome of this is Universal Unfoldment. Furthermore, these various stages / movement patterns equate to what, from the perspective of the observed Universe, human specks of thought/awareness refer to as: non-living (inanimate), living without thought/awareness (plant/fungi), and living with thought/awareness (animal).

The emergence of specks of thought/awareness brings into existence the final stage of the *Stages of Universal Unfoldment.* The purpose of this emergence is to enable the Universal Feeling Body to reach the most intense feeling states of attraction that it is possible to attain. Such lofty states – the highest of high-intensity feelings – would be tragically unattainable in the absence of specks of thought/awareness; for, in this scenario animal bodies (the nodes of feeling that originate high-level feelings in the unobserved Universe) would not be guided and steered so as to flourish and actualise their potentials.

The mapping of human conceptual divisions onto the Universal Feeling Body

You, or I, or other specks of thought/awareness that are situated in human bodies, might conceptually mould a particular bit of the Universal Feeling Body and assert: *this is a tree.* This segment of the Universe is a living entity that is devoid of thought/awareness; therefore, it is a collection of nodes that originate medium-level feelings. That is to say, the intensity of the feelings that the segment of the Universe that humans call a 'tree' can originate is greater than in the segments of the Universe that are non-living, whilst being less intense than those that can be originated in the segments of the Universe that are animal bodies.

Humans visually perceive three types of parts. Those parts which humans visually perceive as non-living (a stone, a saucepan, a helicopter) are collections of nodes of low-level feeling. Those parts which humans visually perceive as living without thought/awareness (a plant, a tree, a mushroom) are collections of nodes of medium-level feeling. Those parts which humans visually perceive as living with thought/awareness (a human, a cat, a dolphin, a seagull) are collections of nodes of high-level feeling. *If you have fully grasped the meaning of the previous paragraph then you will have come to appreciate something that is very important. For, you will now clearly understand that the conceptual divisions in their observed Universes that are created by humans map onto actual concrete differences in the Universal Feeling Body when the concept boundaries a single mode – that which is non-living, or that which is living without thought/awareness, or that which is living with thought/awareness. Whereas, the conceptual divisions in their observed Universes that are created by humans within each of these three modes – non-living, living without thought/awareness, and living with thought/awareness – do not map onto actual concrete differences in the Universal Feeling Body.*

Envision a library when it is closed and contains no living entities. From the perspective of the Universal Feeling Body there are no divisions in the library. There are simply a multitude of nodes of low-level feeling, which participate in an immense plethora of things. Whereas, if I was to visually perceive the library I would create a ginormous number of divisions – there will be thousands upon thousands of 'books', there will be 'bookshelves', 'tables', 'chairs', 'windows', 'walls', 'floor tiles', 'lights', 'light switches', 'doors', 'posters', 'pens', 'newspapers', 'leaflets', 'magazines', 'computers', 'telephones', and so on. That which is one, that which is undivided, is perceptually carved, conceptually carved, into an immense plethora of diverse objects. This means that there is no correspondence between the parts/objects that are visually perceived and concrete differences in the Universal Feeling Body, when all of the conceptually moulded parts are non-living.

Similarly, if a human asserts that a particular segment of the Universe that is living without thought/awareness contains a plethora of parts – a trunk, roots, fifty branches, and two thousand leaves – then there is no correspondence between this plethora of discrete parts and concrete differences in the Universal Feeling Body. In the unobserved Universe this segment of the Universe is simply an undivided originator of medium-level feelings – a multitude of nodes of medium-level feeling, which participate in an immense plethora of things.

The existence of different intensities of feeling in different bits of the Universal Feeling Body means that there are concrete real differences. Yet, it is also the case that these differences do not constitute divisions or boundaries. Within the Universal Feeling Body there are differences in feeling intensity, and in some locations shining beacons exist, but such concrete differences do not create boundaries. The Universal Feeling Body is a boundaryless interconnected matrix of feeling; feeling which is continuously changing, moving, and radiating from its point of origination to that with which it is associated.

The mapping of the conceptual divisions of non-human animals

In the previous section we explored how human conceptual divisions sometimes map onto concrete divisions in the Universal Feeling Body. We need to address the issue of whether this mapping also occurs when non-human animals perceive the Universe.

All animals that have a visual sense conceptually mould that which is visually sensed into parts. For, a visual sense senses the movements of the one giant movement pattern in a particular way, and the speck of thought/awareness in an animal has to interpret these movements and thereby create an observed Universe of parts. Conceptual mouldings are simply these parts. An animal couldn't negotiate its way through its surroundings, and survive, if it didn't have an observed Universe of parts.

Our question here is simply: Do the conceptual mouldings of non-human animals map onto concrete divisions in the Universal Feeling Body? In other words, do the conceptual mouldings of non-human animals map onto the three different levels of feeling nodes, which are the three modes of the Universe? Recall that we earlier explored how all of the animals on the Earth that have a visual sense are medium-grained visual sensors. From this perspective, one can appreciate that what was discussed and concluded in the previous section concerning humans, also applies to non-human animals. That is to say, the conceptual mouldings of all of the medium-grained sensors that have evolved on the Earth will sometimes map onto concrete differences in the Universal Feeling Body: when the conceptual moulding puts a boundary around the unique movement patterns of nodes of feeling from any of the three modes of the Universe. And sometimes this mapping won't occur: when the conceptual moulding establishes a boundary within the movements of collections of nodes of feeling of one of the three modes, rather than around the movement of a particular mode.

Experiencing the Universal Feeling Body

We have seen that the visual sense provides a structured sensing of the effects that emanate from the interactions of nodes of feeling and their things. Furthermore, a speck of thought/awareness can only make sense of the visual sensings that it is presented with by dividing them up into parts. The Universal Feeling Body as a tightly interconnected nexus, as a forever changing singular entity that is comprised of an immense number of networks of feelings overlaying and underlaying networks of feelings, can be envisioned by a speck of thought/awareness. It can be envisioned; but, it cannot be observed. However, the Universal Feeling Body can be experienced directly; for, one is a speck of thought/awareness which has a Universal Feeling Body. One has direct experience of the Universal Feeling Body, because one continuously becomes aware of its existence.

One becomes aware of feelings, feelings that are typically located within one's head, torso, arms, or legs. However, one also regularly becomes aware of feelings that are located in other bits of one's Universal Feeling Body, such as the feelings that are located in one's partner, or one's friends, or one's pets, or the animals that one encounters in a zoo. As we have explored, a speck of thought/awareness can potentially become directly aware of these feelings at their point of origin. And, due to the instant radiation of feelings throughout their things, a speck of thought/awareness can also become aware of such feelings in its animal body. Yet, this is a reality that is very rarely faced up to. For, one is culturally programmed to believe that one is an isolated entity (a 'mind') that is situated within an isolated human body. This means that one naturally assumes that all of the feelings that one becomes aware of both originate within, and exist within, one's own animal body. Yet, the reality is that one is simply a speck of thought/awareness that has a Universal Feeling Body.

In our contemporary stage of Solar-Systic and cultural unfoldment the notion of becoming aware of feelings that either originate outside of one's human body, or exist outside of one's human body, is typically considered 'paranormal'. That is to say, it is something that is currently beyond scientific understanding. This is not surprising; for, science is a very limited endeavour when it comes to appreciating the fundamental nature of the Universe. One cannot come to appreciate the existence and the nature of the Universal Feeling Body through science. However, one can come to appreciate the existence of the Universal Feeling Body through dwelling in one's own experience, through reflecting on one's own experience, and through learning about the experiences of other specks of thought/awareness. Some specks of thought/awareness have had lucid and stark experiences which involve them becoming aware of feelings of intense pain that originated in segments of the Universe that are located outside of the human body in which they are situated. We have already encountered such an example in the section: *# The 3am awakening and the misattribution of feeling.*

 # Two groups of feeling – attraction and repulsion – provide the pathway that is Universal Unfoldment

The phenomenon of pain naturally leads us to reflect upon the idea that all feelings can be divided into two groups – welcome/pleasant/desirable feelings, and unwelcome/unpleasant/undesirable feelings. Our question is: Can the Universal Feeling Body be sharply divided into two portions: feelings that are 'desirable' and feelings that are 'undesirable'? This isn't a straightforward question to answer.

To start with, we can appreciate that the unfolding of the Universal Feeling Body (the evolution of the Universe) is determined and directed by the quality, the intensity, and the location, of the feelings that exist. Biological processes, chemical processes, and physical processes, are all determined and directed by the particular feelings involved. If two feelings are attracted to each other, then they will come together and interact. If two feelings are repulsed by each other, then they will move away from each other. One can fruitfully reflect upon the attractive and repulsive forces of magnetism, as one envisions these forces of feeling attraction and feeling repulsion permeating all of the movements and interactions throughout all of the Universal Feeling Body.

So, it is true to say that there are two very distinct groups of feeling within the Universal Feeling Body: feelings of attraction and feelings of repulsion. However, it would be far too simplistic to take the further step of asserting that feelings of attraction are welcome/pleasant/desirable, whereas feelings of repulsion are unwelcome/unpleasant/undesirable. There is some truth in this assertion. Feelings of attraction are certainly desirable, welcome, and pleasant. However, feelings of repulsion are also necessary, and in many ways are also extremely desirable. For, feelings of repulsion are guides which provide a pathway for a segment of the Universe to attain that which is welcome/pleasant/desirable. When feelings of repulsion are encountered they direct the feeling thing towards an optimal trajectory. This applies to the entire Universal Feeling Body, which means that it applies to the interactions of feelings at various spatial sizes, from miniscule things to enormous things. So, whilst the existence of feelings of repulsion can be said to be desirable, they can simultaneously be said to be unpleasant.

A part is not a thing

Recall that the Universal Feeling Body is constituted out of things (bonds between feelings), whilst the observed Universe is constituted out of parts (the concepts that arise in a speck of thought/awareness). A part can bare some resemblance to things, can roughly map onto things.

For example, a human body is a part in my observed Universe, and this part is simultaneously, in the Universal Feeling Body, a collection of nodes of origination of high-level feeling. Furthermore, as this part contains a collection of feelings that are very deeply embedded, a large proportion of these feelings will be equally-embedded to varying degrees of deepness, and will therefore constitute things that are wholly, or predominantly, located where the human body is located.

So, there is some correspondence between the observed Universe and the state of the Universal Feeling Body. However, whilst a human body is a part, it is not a thing; for, a thing is not a delineated boundaried entity. Things are bonds, associations, between feelings. A thing is a network, an interconnected web. A human body contains an immense plethora of things, and a human body participates in an immense plethora of things; it isn't itself a thing. One cannot visually perceive a particular bit of one's observed Universe (a part) and meaningfully assert: *this is a thing.*

Feelings of repulsion

One can easily comprehend how one's own actions/movements are determined by feelings of attraction and feelings of repulsion. Let us start by considering feelings of repulsion. If one becomes aware of feelings of extreme pain in one's human body this will, no doubt, determine one's actions/movements; typically, one will act in a way which aims to eliminate these feelings of repulsion. If one has burnt one's hand, one is likely to put the hand under cold running water. If one has twisted one's ankle, one is likely to put an ice pack on it. If one has a headache, one is likely to take a paracetamol tablet. If one has extreme chest pain, one is likely to go to the hospital. If one has a piercing toothache, one is likely to contact the dentist, or take other actions to address the pain. Whilst, if one smells something that is repugnant, one is likely to move away from it. If one tastes something that is vile, one is likely to spit it out. And, if one hears something that is painfully dissonant and jarring, then one is likely to cover one's ears. In all of these ways, feelings of repulsion direct one's actions/movements in a way that is helpful, valuable, and conducive to one's future survival and wellbeing.

Feelings of attraction

Let us turn to an exploration of feelings of attraction. One is highly likely to become aware of feelings of attraction on a regular basis throughout the day. When one becomes aware of such feelings, one will simultaneously become aware of the actions/movements of one's human body that seem to accompany these feelings. In the past, one will have become aware of the feelings that came into existence when one's human body undertook a wide variety of actions/movements. This awareness constitutes knowledge of the feelings that are highly likely to come into existence when one's human body undertakes particular actions/movements. Consequently, such knowledge is a causal factor in determining one's actions/movements in the present.

One might know that one enjoys the feelings that come into existence when one's human body drinks a cup of coffee, or a pint of lager, so this causes one to go to the café or to the pub. One might know that one's human body has feelings of exhilaration at classical music concerts, or at a football match, so this causes one to go to a classical music concert or a football match. One might know that one's human body has feelings of attraction – welcome/pleasant/desirable feelings – when sunbathing on the beach, doing voluntary work, watching a particular television programme, spending time with a friend, playing the piano, walking the dog, doing a jigsaw, going for a run, going to work, hugging a tree, doing a yoga class, driving one's car, or spending time in a forest. So, one decides to do these activities.

 # Feelings of attraction and repulsion are specific to particular parts

Feelings of attraction and feelings of repulsion permeate the Universal Feeling Body – they are the domain of nodes and their things. The parts of one's observed Universe are not nodes or things, but we can still sensibly talk about the feelings of attraction and repulsion that exist in the parts that constitute one's observed Universe. Indeed, when we consider one's observed Universe it is very important to appreciate that feelings of attraction and repulsion are specific to particular parts. For example, some human bodies will have feelings of attraction whilst taking a dog for a walk, whereas other human bodies will have feelings of repulsion whilst taking a dog for a walk. If your human body experiences feelings of repulsion around dogs, then you are unlikely to take a dog for a walk; rather, when you encounter a dog you will attempt to keep your distance. Similarly, going to Berry Pomeroy Castle, going to a yoga class, and watching a particular television programme, can result in feelings of repulsion for some human bodies, and feelings of attraction for other human bodies.

One might encounter a novel situation in the course of one's day and one's human body might unexpectedly be overcome with a particular type of feeling. Such an occurrence will play a role in determining one's actions in the proceeding moments, and also in the following years and decades of one's life. For example, the first time that one goes on a rollercoaster, or goes skydiving, or goes abseiling, or starts to knit, or goes surfing, or plays short-mat bowls, or goes for a sauna, then one might be surprised when one's human body becomes overwhelmed with welcome/pleasant/desirable feelings. This experience is highly likely to cause one to continue doing this activity, and also to do this activity again and again in the future. Of course, if one of these activities were to result in one becoming aware of feelings of repulsion, then one is likely to immediately stop doing this activity, and to avoid such an activity in the future.

The movements of the Universal Feeling Body – the currantless bun

The movements of the Universal Feeling Body are overwhelmingly determined and directed by feelings. Envision the Universe, at a time in the distant past, when there were no specks of thought/awareness. This is the state of the Universe that we have previously referred to as 'the currantless bun'. In this state of the Universe, the Universal Feeling Body exists as an unobserved matrix of intricately interconnected overlapping networks of things. All of the movements within the currantless bun are wholly and automatically determined by the feeling states that exist.

The movements of the Universal Feeling Body – specks of thought/awareness

When specks of thought/awareness exist in the Universal Feeling Body, these specks emerge within networks of things. The decisions of these specks of thought/awareness can initiate movements, movements whose feeling impacts are felt throughout the networks of things within which the movement occurs. Recall that we earlier explored the distinction between direct and indirect movements. The direct movements that are initiated by a speck of thought/awareness are movements of its animal body that affect the feelings of its entire Universal Feeling Body. Indirect movements are very varied, but their commonality is that they only exist because of the decisions and actions of a speck of thought/awareness.

In the currantless bun every single movement is wholly and automatically determined by the feeling states that currently exist. Now, in the year 2024, there are an immense plethora of specks of thought/awareness on the Earth that are initiating both direct and indirect movements. These movements change the feeling in that which moves. They also lead to feeling radiating throughout the things in which the movement occurs, thereby modifying the feeling throughout these things. A question that we need to address is: Does the radiation of feeling that is caused by direct and indirect movements affect the movements of the segments of the Universe that the feeling is radiated to? This is a subset of the question: Does the radiation of feeling affect movement?

Whilst specks of thought/awareness can fruitfully be envisioned as currants that initiate direct and indirect movements and thereby cause feelings to be radiated throughout things, it is important to appreciate that the intensity of this feeling varies drastically in accordance with both the degree of embeddedness of particular things, and the feeling intensity of the nodes in particular things. We have explored how the combination, the interplay, of these two factors creates deeply feeling things and weakly feeling things.

When movements are initiated in deeply feeling things, the radiating feelings that are generated can be pivotal in determining movement, but they can also play no role in determining movement; it depends on the specifics of a particular situation. If the movement generates the most intense feeling in a deeply feeling thing, then the feeling will dominate the thing and thus potentially play a key role in determining the movement of the segments of the Universe where the thing exists. I say 'potentially' because a particular segment of the Universe will participate in a plethora of things, and its movement will be determined by the aggregate feeling effects of all of these things, along with any possible influences from a speck of thought/awareness. This means that each specific situation will involve a different role in generating movement for a radiating feeling that is generated in a deeply feeling thing by a direct or indirect movement – from pivotal to inconsequential.

In contrast, when movements are initiated in weakly feeling things the feelings that are radiated will be extremely low-level feelings. This means that they will not affect the movement of the segments of the Universe that are radiated to; for, these radiating feelings will be dwarfed by the much more intense feelings that exist in the more deeply feeling things that exist in particular locations.

The movements of the Universal Feeling Body – the steering of the animal body

A speck of thought/awareness has the precious ability to make decisions, to reflect, to ponder, and to take alternative possible courses of action. How wonderful this is! This ability enables a speck of thought/awareness to steer and guide its animal body, in order to enable it to flourish and thereby to instantiate increasingly welcome/pleasant/desirable feelings. A speck can also make flawed decisions / mistakes; these are decisions which initiate actions that inadvertently cause unwelcome/unpleasant feelings to come into existence. In this way, feelings are a guide which let a speck of thought/awareness know that it has made a bad decision. Of course, from the perspective of the Universal Feeling Body, to say that a speck of thought/awareness is steering and guiding its animal body, is to say that it is steering and guiding a collection of nodes of high-level feeling; nodes that are participants in an immense plethora of things in the borderless unobserved Universe.

The movements of the Universal Feeling Body – conclusion

Feelings determine all of the movements of the overwhelming majority of the Universal Feeling Body. Where specks of thought/awareness exist, feelings act as a guide which enables those specks of thought/awareness to make increasingly good decisions concerning the future health and wellbeing of the animal bodies within which they intermittently emerge. Furthermore, such decisions do not only affect animal bodies; they also affect Universal Feeling Bodies; for, as we earlier explored, the direct movements that are initiated by a speck of thought/awareness have feeling affects throughout its Universal Feeling Body.

In addition to initiating direct movements, specks of thought/awareness can also initiate indirect movements – such as putting a satellite into orbit, or causing a drone to fly through the sky – and such movements have become an increasingly important source of movement on the Earth. Such movements have a ripple effect; as they occur they bring feelings into being, feelings that instantly radiate throughout their things.

A cascade of feeling is brought into being. Indeed, through bringing into existence enormous numbers of indirect movements, one can envision specks of thought/awareness as shepherds of feeling, as architects of feeling, who are gathering up nodes of feeling, and channelling them into particular novel arrangements.

The purpose of human existence

There is something much deeper going on here; something profound. *For, when specks of thought/awareness make increasingly good decisions concerning the future health and wellbeing of their animal bodies, they are, of necessity, making decisions that ensure the future wellbeing of the Universe.* If one fully comprehends this, comes to know the reality that these words are describing, then one will be fast approaching the deepest levels of wisdom, the deepest insights, that it is possible to attain concerning the nature of the Universe and the purpose of human existence. One will be able to behold the fundamental nature of all that is; one will be able to behold the inevitably unfolding trajectory of our evolving Solar System; and, one will be able to behold the purpose of the human species within this process of cosmic unfolding.

The flourishing of individual human bodies

Of course, human bodies are individuals; they are all different. What is a trajectory of health and wellbeing for one human body is likely to be different to what is a trajectory of health and wellbeing for another human body. The feelings that a particular speck of thought/awareness becomes aware of, when its animal body moves in particular ways, are a unique guide to health and wellbeing for the animal body within which that speck of thought/awareness is situated; for, whilst some human bodies are quite similar to each other in terms of their personality, passions, abilities, skills, and aptitudes, some human bodies are starkly different in terms of these attributes.

We have explored how the quality and the intensity of the feelings that a speck of thought/awareness becomes aware of are its most precious tool. These feelings aid a speck of thought/awareness in its endeavour to set the human body within which it intermittently emerges onto a life trajectory of increasingly pleasant/desirable feelings. What are sought are actions which match passions in accordance with personality, actions which match abilities, skills, and aptitudes. Success in this endeavour – a very high level of matching – creates a fulfilling life trajectory, a flourishing human body. This life trajectory entails a specific path which enables a particular human body to maximise its potential, and thereby become an immensely precious and valuable segment of the Universe.

The actualisation of potentials throughout the Universe

Every human body is different. Every human body is a unique collection of feelings; feelings of a particular quality. Every human body is a unique collection of passions, personality and abilities/skills/aptitudes. To talk of 'personality' in an animal body is to talk of its essence – the way that it needs to move in order to flourish. These words are a crude attempt to point towards that which differentiates one human body from another human body. Such differentiation is that which causes divergent feelings to come into existence in different human bodies when these bodies move in particular ways, and thereby is that which causes specks to initiate actions that result in human bodies living their lives differently. All of this also applies to non-human animal bodies and their specks of thought/awareness. Furthermore, in respect to all of this, animal bodies are not significantly different from the rest of the Universe.

Every segment of the Universe has both a particular feeling quality and particular abilities/skills/aptitudes. That is to say, every segment of the Universe has the potential to move in particular ways, and thereby to feel in particular ways, and in the right circumstances these segments realise this potentiality. So, the actualisation of potentials entails the coming into being of particular feelings. We can say that every segment of the Universe has 'personality'/'passions' due to the particular way that it interacts with that which is not itself. The term 'personality' points at the potentiality that a segment of the Universe has to deploy certain abilities/skills/aptitudes; whilst, the term 'passions' points at the feelings of attraction that accompany this deployment. So, this means that the former term points at the Universe, whilst the latter term points solely at the unobserved Universe – the Universal Feeling Body.

The dynamic interplay between feelings, specks of thought/awareness, and abilities/skills/aptitudes

Let us focus on animal bodies. What makes animal bodies different from the vast majority of the Universe is simply that in addition to the feelings and abilities/skills/aptitudes that pervade the Universe, animal bodies sometimes contain a speck of thought/awareness.

A speck of thought/awareness arises in the brain of an animal body, but it has a Universal Feeling Body. The animal body is a part in an observed Universe – a boundaried entity that is conceptually moulded by a speck of thought/awareness. *Where a speck of thought/awareness exists there is a dynamic interplay between itself, abilities/skills/aptitudes, and feelings.*

Feelings are directly related to abilities/skills/aptitudes. For, when a human body, any animal body, or any other segment of the Universe, is utilising its abilities/skills/aptitudes, then pleasant/desirable feelings come into existence. Whilst, when an animal body is acting in a way that is not conducive to the utilisation of its abilities/skills/aptitudes – acting against its personality – then unpleasant/undesirable feelings come into existence. Furthermore, the actions of an animal body typically arise from the decisions of that body's speck of thought/awareness.

So, the decisions of a speck of thought/awareness lead to actions, and these actions either will or will not utilise abilities/skills/aptitudes. These actions also bring certain feelings into existence – either feelings of attraction or feelings of repulsion. And, to complete the interplay, these feelings affect, inform, constrain, and direct, the decision-making process of a speck of thought/awareness.

Autopilot

In order to deepen one's understanding of the relationship between feelings, specks of thought/awareness, and abilities/skills/aptitudes, it is fruitful to consider the phenomenon of 'autopilot'. The actions of a human body, and of any other animal body, are typically determined by their speck of thought/awareness. I say 'typically' because there are fairly frequent occasions when animal bodies act on autopilot in the absence of a speck of thought/awareness.

In these situations an animal body is moving, feelings exist in the animal body, parts can be visually perceived, and feelings can be auditorily sensed by the ears and recognised as auditory outputs, yet the speck of thought/awareness in the animal body is not present. The speck of thought/awareness has temporarily vanished. In these moments there are seemingly actions, with certain abilities/skills/aptitudes being deployed, but there is no 'I' instigating the actions. As there is no 'I' in these actions, it is debatable whether they should actually be called 'actions'; perhaps the movements of the animal body should just be called 'movements of the Universe'.

Feelings guide actions

The actions of human bodies, and of non-human animal bodies, are typically determined by their speck of thought/awareness. A speck becomes aware of the feelings that come into existence when its animal body acts in a particular way. And, this awareness of the quality and intensity of the feelings which accompany bodily actions is the guide which enables a speck of thought/awareness to make decisions – within the bounds of the abilities/skills/aptitudes of its animal body – that are conducive to the welfare and wellbeing of that body.

Decisions which result in actions that utilise the abilities/skills/aptitudes of the animal body, whilst also being in accordance with its personality, lead to flourishing; such actions are inevitably accompanied by feelings of attraction: pleasant/desirable feelings; for, the passions of the animal body are actualised. In contrast, all other actions are accompanied by feelings of repulsion in the animal body: unpleasant/undesirable feelings.

In this way, the actions of human bodies, and the actions of the bodies of other animals, can actually be seen to be fundamentally determined by feelings, rather than by a speck of thought/awareness. For, a speck of thought/awareness is strongly naturally disposed to make decisions, to initiate actions, which result in pleasant/desirable feelings, and to steer away from decisions and actions that it knows, or believes, will result in unpleasant/undesirable feelings.

The diverse range of expressions of the Universal Feeling Body

Every human body, every animal body, is unique. This means that every speck of thought/awareness will have a unique feeling guide. In other words, the actions that result in one animal body flourishing will be different to the actions that result in another animal body flourishing. Why is this? Why are human bodies all different in this way? Why are the bodies of non-human animals all different in this way? Our answer: every animal body is a unique expression of the Universal Feeling Body.

As a singular borderless entity, the Universal Moving Body / the Universal Feeling Body has within it a diverse range of expressions, a distinct number of sides that are regularly brought forth into existence in a cyclical fashion. This range of expressions equates to the different sets of personalities/abilities/skills/aptitudes that are forged in human bodies, that are forged in the bodies of non-human animals, and that are forged in every other segment of the Universe, as these segments are brought forth into existence as a unique expression of the Universal Feeling Body.

The cyclical nature of the bringing forth of human bodies with distinct personalities/abilities/skills/aptitudes, is a phenomenon that astrologers have been seeking to understand for thousands of years. On the one hand, there is uniqueness, complete individuality. On the other hand, there are groupings of similar individuals, with each grouping being one of the diverse range of expressions of the Universal Feeling Body.

The feeling state of the Solar-Systic whole

If one is to fully appreciate the causes of the states of feeling that exist in animal bodies, and the causes of the states of feeling that exist in all segments of our Solar System, then one needs to consider the positions of our Solar-Systic planets within the Universe. Each of the planets in our Solar System is a shining beacon within the Universal Feeling Body. That is to say, each of the planets is a location of extremely deeply embedded feeling of a particular quality. The arrangement of these planets – their relative positions within our Solar System – corresponds to feelings of a particular quality coming into existence and dominating our Solar System for particular periods of time. For, a particular arrangement of planets is a particular arrangement of feeling.

I imagine that it is probably not very clear to you what I am attempting to convey here. For, envisioning, and coming to know, the planets of our Solar System as collections of feelings, whose locations vis-à-vis each other creates a collective Solar-Systic feeling state, is not a familiar way of thinking about our Solar System. We can fruitfully get a handle on the existence of the feeling state of the Solar-Systic whole by envisioning something more familiar, such as a headache.

You can envision your headache as a particular arrangement of the Universe, a particular movement pattern that is located in your head. This particular arrangement, like every other segment of the Universe, is a movement pattern of feelings. If this particular arrangement of feelings exists, then you will have a headache. There will be feelings of discomfort filling one's head. However, when this movement pattern of feelings in your head changes in a particular way, then the headache will cease. In a similar way, you can envision a particular arrangement of planets in our Solar System equating to a Solar-Systic headache. This involves feelings of discomfort and unease filling large swathes of our Solar System. When the planets move into a different feeling arrangement, a different movement pattern, then the Solar-Systic headache ceases.

As the planets move, the feelings of the Earth change; these feelings include the bodies of animals. So, the movements of the planets can change the feelings of both the body of a mother, and the body of the baby that is in her womb. Furthermore, these changing feelings can cause the mother to act/move in a particular way, thereby further changing both her feelings and the feelings of the baby that is in her womb.

We are talking about ginormous collections of feelings (planets) having feeling effects that permeate the entire Solar System as they come into particular arrangements. We are talking about a particular feeling state of the feeling Solar-Systic whole. To put it rather crudely, one could say that from the perspective of the Universal Feeling Body as a whole, our

Solar System was in, say, 'a state of discomfort', or that, alternatively, it was in 'a state of ecstasy'. How does the feeling state of the Solar-Systic whole relate to the formation of things? That is, how does it relate to particular nodes of feeling becoming embedded with each other and thereby instantly co-radiating feeling to each other to an extent that is dependent upon the degree of embeddedness of a particular thing? We will return to this question later.

The feeling state of the Solar-Systic whole is the existence of a particular type of qualitative state which defines the current state of our Solar System. One can very fruitfully directly relate these qualitative states to epochs in the unfolding of human culture. For instance, the feeling state of the Solar-Systic whole is currently, in the year 2024, in 'a state of discomfort'. In the realm of human cultural unfoldment on the Earth this state is instantiated in human bodies in terms of a sense of unease, purposelessness, antagonism, desperation, conflict, and despair.

The ingestion and digestion of feelings

Let us now turn to a consideration of food and drink. The food and drink that human bodies, and other animal bodies, ingest and digest are, of course, collections of feelings of a particular quality and intensity. Animal bodies ingest and digest feelings, and some of these feelings merge with pre-existing bodily feelings and thereby become a highly significant part of the animal body. So, ingested nodes of feeling can become a speck of thought/awareness's close travelling companion.

You might want to pause and reflect upon what you are ingesting and digesting in your human body. Reflect not upon calories, fat content, sugar content, protein, fibre, vitamins, and minerals. Reflect upon the feelings that you are ingesting and digesting. Reflect upon the history of that which you are ingesting and digesting. For, embedded within feelings are memories. Every feeling has a history. Every feeling tells a story. You are ingesting and digesting histories and stories, and these become absorbed into your human body. These histories and stories, these memories, become very significant components of both your close travelling companion, and your Universal Feeling Body.

Pain and suffering – the poisoned chalice of the gift that is thought/awareness

You do not really want to be ingesting nodes of feeling that are saturated with feelings of intense pain and suffering. This is not good for you. Feelings of pain and suffering become feeling memories of pain and suffering. Such feelings are stifling and can be seeds of contagion within the animal body; the diffusing of feeling memories of pain and suffering. How can you avoid, or at least minimise, ingesting and digesting nodes of feeling that are saturated with feeling memories of pain and suffering? To answer this question we simply need to explore which segments of the Universe can be 'in pain' / suffer.

There is a stark division here; a division that is easy to comprehend. For there to be an entity that is 'in pain' / suffering, there has to be a speck of thought/awareness. To be 'in pain' and to suffer requires an 'I'. And an 'I' is nothing more than a speck of thought/awareness. Those segments of the Universe that lack a speck of thought/awareness cannot be 'in pain', cannot suffer. Furthermore, those segments of the Universe that lack a speck of thought/awareness cannot originate high-level feelings, let alone high intensity feelings. Pain and suffering is the domain of a speck of thought/awareness and its animal body; it is the poisoned chalice of the gift that is thought/awareness.

 # An exploration of pain and suffering in the Universe

We need to delve a little deeper into the realm of pain and suffering. The unobserved Universe only contains movement patterns of feelings, and possibly also specks of thought/awareness, with these specks having an occasional and intermittent existence. Feelings have a particular qualitative nature and they can be divided into feelings of attraction and feelings of repulsion. Feelings of pain are intense feelings of repulsion. Feelings of pain exist irrespective of whether or not a speck is aware of their existence. A speck of thought/awareness is a qualityless window. If a speck of thought/awareness becomes aware of feelings of pain then it will be 'in pain', and it will possibly also be suffering. There needs to be awareness for the notions of suffering and being 'in pain' to make any sense. Feelings cannot become aware of themselves. Only a speck of thought/awareness can suffer, can be 'in pain'.

Pain is nothing more than a feeling. Being 'in pain' is being aware of this feeling. The feelings of repulsion in Mode 1 and Mode 2 segments of the Universe are not intense enough to warrant the label 'pain'. If the feeling of pain that a speck of thought/awareness becomes aware of is intense enough then it will inevitably suffer. Mild pain does not cause suffering to a speck of thought/awareness. Suffering is a much more complex phenomenon than pain. Bodily pain can cause a speck of thought/awareness to suffer. However, there is another vicious cause of suffering. For, a speck of thought/awareness can bring suffering to itself. You will recall that the purpose of a speck of thought/awareness is to steer and guide its animal body in order to enable that animal body to flourish, to actualise its potentials, to utilise its abilities/skills/aptitudes. If a speck is prohibited from doing this then the outcome is extremely likely to be a state of anguish, of agonising frustration, of despair, where negative thought patterns increasingly originate, propagate, spiral, and escalate. These negative spirals of thought entail suffering for a speck of thought/awareness.

Suffering from negative thought spirals

It will be fruitful to consider some scenarios in which negative thought spirals are highly likely to develop. So, envision a bird that is imprisoned within a small cage. The speck of thought/awareness that is located in the bird's body is desperate to actualise the potentials of the animal body; it wants to propel the bird to fly majestically through the sky. Yet, it is cruelly prohibited from doing so. The thought patterns of the bird enter a negative spiral of anguish, deflation, desperation, and frustration. The speck of thought/awareness suffers.

In a similar vein, you can envision animals that are subjects of vivisection, and also battery hens that are imprisoned in battery cages. The specks of thought/awareness that are situated in the bodies of these animals are prohibited from fulfilling their role of enabling their animal bodies to actualise their potentials, and this leads to an increasingly negative spiral of thought patterns deep into the depths of anguish and despair. These specks of thought/awareness are suffering.

Let us now envision a human body that has been wrongfully imprisoned for life, cruelly sent to jail for a crime that it did not commit. The speck of thought/awareness that is located in this body is powerless to actualise the potentials of the body. It is haunted by the unjustness and unfairness of the situation. Its thought patterns can all too easily enter a vicious downwards spiral of negative thought leading to even more negative thought. In this situation, the speck of thought/awareness is suffering.

In all of the examples that we have considered there are two different sources of suffering. Firstly, the speck of thought/awareness is suffering due to negative spirals of thought which emanate from its inability to actualise the potentials of its animal body. Secondly, the speck suffers due to the coming into being of feelings of pain/repulsion in its animal body. For, if an animal body doesn't, for whatever reason, actualise its potential, then the outcome is feelings of pain in the animal body.

*# The lawnmower and the distinctive types of movement in the Universal
Feeling Body*

It will be fruitful for us to consider the activity of using a lawnmower to
cut grass. What is a lawnmower? A lawnmower is simultaneously a part
in my observed Universe, a segment of the Universe, and a conceptual
moulding of the movements of the Universal Feeling Body. A lawnmower
is conceptually moulded, segregated from its surroundings, by an entity
that understands that a lawnmower is a machine that cuts grass. In the
unobserved Universe, the activity of a lawnmower cutting grass is just
that – an activity, a particular type of movement within the 'one giant
movement pattern'; this is, of course, a movement which involves the
origination of particular types of feeling.

The Universal Feeling Body is continuously in a state of movement
throughout itself. What a human might call the activity of 'cutting grass'
is simply some movement in a tiny bit of the Universal Feeling Body,
movement that has been conceptually isolated. If we so wished, we
could call this particular type of movement: 'lawnmower movement'. It is
a distinctive type of movement, that is very different from these types of
movement: 'airplane movement', 'car movement', 'worm movement',
'helicopter movement', 'seagull movement', 'squirrel movement', 'tree
movement', 'water movement', and 'human movement'.

The segment of the Universe that some specks conceptually mould as 'a
lawnmower' is a collection of nodes of low-level feelings. The grass that
is cut is a collection of nodes of medium-level feelings. For the grass,
growing is a state of flourishing, a state of actualising its potential; being
cut is the opposite. Thus one can envision that prior to being cut there
are feelings of attraction in the grass, and that the act of cutting brings
into being feelings of repulsion. Of course, grass does not contain a speck
of thought/awareness; so, it cannot be 'in pain', it cannot suffer.

The storage of thought

We have been pondering the negative spirals of thought that typically come into existence when a speck of thought/awareness is prohibited from actualising the potentials in its animal body. The question before us now is: Do these thoughts become stored in the Universal Feeling Body? Our answer is 'yes': thoughts become stored in nodes of feeling. Thoughts will become stored as memories in nodes of feeling if there is a very high level of embeddedness between a speck of thought/awareness and these nodes of feeling. This means that, in terms of the observed Universe, these thoughts will typically be stored in the animal body in which a speck of thought/awareness intermittently emerges.

Feelings of pain versus being 'in pain'

Let us say a little more about the distinction between feelings of pain and being 'in pain'. Feelings of repulsion need to be above a certain level of intensity before it makes sense to say that these feelings are feelings of pain. These would be feelings that are intense enough that if a speck of thought/awareness became aware of them, then they would assert that they were 'in pain'. In order for there to be suffering, the feelings of pain that a speck of thought/awareness becomes aware of need to either be extremely intense, or to be of a lesser intensity that exists for a prolonged period of time.

Only a speck of thought/awareness can be 'in pain'; only a speck of thought/awareness can suffer. Furthermore, the feelings of pain, the feelings which can cause a speck of thought/awareness to be 'in pain', and to suffer, originate in the collections of nodes of high-level feeling that are animal bodies. For, whilst nodes of medium-level feeling (that which is living without thought/awareness) often instantiate feelings of repulsion, these feelings are much less intense than high-level feelings. Such feelings, if a speck of thought/awareness were to become aware of them, are likely to result in an assertion of being 'in a state of slight unease', rather than being 'in pain'.

Ingesting animals versus ingesting plants

It will be useful for us to draw together some threads in order to consider the difference between ingesting animals and ingesting plants (what is said here concerning plants also applies to fungi). Whatever one ingests, one will be ingesting feelings. And, feelings come in two types: feelings of repulsion, and feelings of attraction. These two types of feelings exist in both animals and plants. When they are growing, when they are alive, plants are collections of nodes of medium-level feelings. In contrast, the living animal body is a collection of nodes of high-level feelings. This is an important difference; however, the major difference between plants and animals is the presence of a speck of thought/awareness. A speck of thought/awareness emerges in animal bodies, emerges in the brains of animals. In other words, the movement pattern of high-level feelings that is an animal brain is that which generates a speck of thought/awareness. Furthermore, only a speck of thought/awareness can be 'in pain' / suffer. Due to the extremely high level of association that exists, the feelings of pain that a speck of thought/awareness becomes aware of are typically located in the animal body – for example, the head, torso, arms, and legs, of a human body – that it is situated within.

We have explored how the source of suffering can either be things or a speck of thought/awareness itself. So, a speck of thought/awareness can become aware of feelings of extreme pain that are not caused by itself. And, a speck of thought/awareness can descend into distressing negative thought spirals when it is not actualising the potentials of its animal body; furthermore, this failure to actualise also results in feelings of pain in the animal body. Additionally, we have explored how thoughts, including tormented thoughts, become stored in the nodes of feeling that constitute an animal body.

So, what are the main differences between ingesting animals and plants? In short, if one ingests animals then one is ingesting much more of a complex thing. The life-history of an animal is effectively embedded into its body parts. Feeling memories, feelings of pain and suffering, will be embedded in the body parts of an animal. Significant pain and suffering is to be expected; for, in the life of an animal, it is par for the course. The more that an animal has suffered, the more intense these feelings will be. The thoughts of the speck of thought/awareness of an animal will also be stored in its body, and these thoughts might well be of a distressing and tormented nature. This will be at its most extreme in the case of factory farmed animals, as their specks of thought/awareness have been continuously prevented from actualising the potentials of their animal bodies; these bodies will thus contain both a torrent of tormented thoughts, and the associated feeling memories of bodily pain that emanate from the failure to actualise.

The situation is very different when it comes to plants. When one ingests the feelings that are a plant, one is ingesting something that is much simpler. In general, if one ingests a plant then one is ingesting relatively pure feeling; whereas, if one ingests an animal then one is likely to be ingesting, digesting, and absorbing into one's animal body, an epicentre of pain and suffering. And, there is truth in the saying: 'what one eats, one becomes'.

What do you think about ingesting and digesting the body parts of an animal that had been in a state of almost perpetual pain and suffering throughout its life? Do you relish the prospect of being able to ingest and digest the body parts of an animal that had spent its life as a subject of vivisection? Do you like the idea of ingesting and digesting the body parts of an animal that had spent its life living in cramped conditions as a subject of modern-day factory farming?

Fruits/vegetables/nuts/fungi – waning feeling intensity and waning feeling purity

When fruits/vegetables/nuts/fungi are growing, when they are alive, when they are Mode 2 segments of the Universe, then they are medium-level feelings. When they are picked, when they cease to be a living segment of the Universe, then their level of feeling inevitably starts to wane, to fade, into the realm of low-level feeling. In other words, the feelings that are fruits/vegetables/nuts/fungi are at their most intense when they are growing, and at the moment of picking. The process of waning feeling intensity following being picked is typically accompanied by a process of waning feeling purity.

Fruits/vegetables/nuts/fungi that have just been picked are typically very pure medium-level feelings. The longer they have been picked, as their feeling intensity gradually fades, fruits/vegetables/nuts/fungi tend to be handled by multiple humans, to be transported in lorries/ships/airplanes, to be frozen, dried, canned and pickled, to be put into cans, boxes, and bags, and to be surrounded by innumerable swarms of human bodies in supermarkets. These are all feeling interactions which reduce the purity of the feelings that are the fruits/vegetables/nuts/fungi.

As time inevitably passes, as the picked fruits/vegetables/nuts/fungi become increasingly handled and surrounded by multiple human bodies, their feelings become increasingly modified, as they become a forever increasing receptacle for human feeling memories. Feeling memories of various qualities/natures, including pain and suffering, increasingly reduce the purity of that which is ultimately ingested and digested. This means that there is clearly an obvious benefit to be had from ingesting and digesting fruits/vegetables/nuts/fungi that have very recently been picked. For, one will benefit from ingesting and digesting a much greater purity of feeling.

Meat – waning feeling intensity and increasing feeling purity

The living animal is a collection of nodes of high-level feeling, but at the moment of its death these feelings gradually wane, gradually fade, into the realm of low-level feelings. If one ingests a just-killed animal one will, to all intents and purposes, be ingesting high-level feelings; whereas, if one ingests animal flesh from tins purchased in a supermarket, then one will almost certainly be ingesting low-level feelings.

We have seen that as time passes after being picked, the feeling purity of fruits/vegetables/nuts/fungi typically steadily wanes. The opposite is true when it comes to animals/meat. For, the living animal is extremely unpure feeling – a jam-packed epicentre of feeling memories of pain, suffering, more wholesome feelings, negative thought spirals, and a plethora of diverse memories. If one ingests and digests a just-killed animal, then this is what one is absorbing into one's animal body. When a living animal ceases to live, when a Mode 3 segment perishes, then the passing of time entails the gradual destruction of this jam-packed epicentre. The rich history of feeling memory starts to wane, to fade, and the feeling purity of the meat consequently increases.

Ingestion and digestion – two conclusions

There are two conclusions that we can draw. Our first conclusion is that it is advisable to ingest fruits/vegetables/nuts/fungi that have just been picked. Our second conclusion is that if one is to ingest meat, then it is best to eat the meat from an animal that died a very long time ago.

Dairy and eggs

Does what has been said concerning meat also apply to dairy and eggs? Yes, it does. However, in the case of dairy and eggs all of the feeling effects are very significantly dampened. For, meat is a deeply embedded jam-packed epicentre of feeling memories, whilst dairy and eggs have a fairly speedy transitory journey through animal bodies. Nevertheless, the same conclusion holds: if one is to ingest dairy and eggs, then it is best to eat the dairy and eggs that exited from an animal body a very long time ago. From a practical perspective, the longer ago the exit, the more preferable this is. So, we are talking about the desirability of eggs that have been pickled, and milk that has been frozen.

In practice, the situation is a little more complex than has been outlined so far. For, if the pickled eggs and frozen milk are stored in a warehouse, or a supermarket, and are continuously surrounded by swarms of human bodies, then there will be an obvious counterbalancing factor. As time passes, feeling purity will initially increase, but as dairy and eggs aren't exorbitantly unpure to start with, the trend towards increasing feeling purity over time can be offset by the interactions with human bodies which reduce feeling purity. The overall outcome can thus be that after a period of time the feeling purity of dairy and eggs starts to wane.

Sites of deeply embedded feeling versus sites of scattered feeling

Our consideration of ingesting and digesting feelings naturally leads us into an exploration of a very important aspect of the Universal Feeling Body; this is the distinction between sites of deeply embedded feeling and sites of scattered feeling. Imagine going into a church that had been constructed a thousand years ago. Imagine that all of the materials that constitute the fabric of the church – the walls, the floor, the ceiling, and the spire – have been in place for a thousand years. Imagine every service that has occurred in this building over the thousand years since it was built. Imagine the feelings generated by the humans in the church as they sing, as they pray, as they rejoice in God. One can easily appreciate how this church has become a site of deeply embedded feeling – deeply embedded feeling of a particular quality. If one were to spend time in this church it would not be surprising if one were to become aware of this deeply embedded feeling. Being in the church will certainly affect you; for, being there will leave a significant feeling imprint on your human body.

Such a church, such an encounter, can be contrasted with a church that was built a week ago, or a month ago. The more recent the construction, the less embedded the feelings that exist there will be. This church is not a site of deeply embedded feeling. It is a site of scattered feeling, which is not pervaded and saturated by feelings of a particular quality. If one goes into this church one is unlikely to become aware of the feelings that are present in the location. Furthermore, these feelings will not leave a significant imprint on one's human body, as compared to when one entered the thousand-year-old church.

One can take the example of the two churches and apply it to the rest of the Universal Feeling Body. Envision the feelings that might overcome one when one enters a 'haunted house'. It is extremely unlikely that the house that one has entered is a new-build construction which was completed the previous week – a site of scattered feeling. It is much more likely that one has entered an ancient building, a very old house, a site with bags of history – a site of deeply embedded feeling.

Envision the feelings that exist in an ancient tree, or ancient woodland, as compared to the feelings that exist in a newly planted tree or a newly planted forest. We have here a stark contrast between sites of deeply embedded feeling and sites of scattered feeling. When one encounters an ancient tree one is encountering deeply embedded nodes of feeling, deeply embedded things, and one's human body might well be overcome with a particular feeling – exuberant feelings of attraction. In contrast, being in the newly planted forest is likely to be a rather empty, soulless, vacuous experience; an experience that fails to make a significant feeling mark on one's human body.

As a tree ages, so does a human. As the years come and go a human body has feelings, becomes a site of feelings, that are less scattered and more embedded. *'What we feel, we become'.* We become what we feel, and what we feel we increasingly become. An increasingly embedded epicentre of feeling, within the Universal Feeling Body, that is guided by the speck of thought/awareness that intermittently emerges from within.

An exploration of various phenomena

The distinction between sites of deeply embedded feeling and sites of scattered feeling, along with the notion of 'flows of feeling', can fruitfully be used to consider particular phenomena that exist in the Universe. In the following sections various phenomena will be explored, from fire and water, to storms, planets, phantom limbs, bulldozers, sunlight, radio waves, helicopters, and human cultural evolution.

Fire, earthquakes, hurricanes, bulldozers and nuclear bombs

Let us consider the phenomenon of fire. Fire is an extremely voracious destroyer of embedded feeling and creator of scattered feeling. The situation is similar, although the destruction/creation is typically less voracious, when it comes to phenomena such as earthquakes, storms, hurricanes, tsunamis, and tornadoes. And the same can be said for sticks of dynamite, bulldozers, and grenades. The most voracious destroyer of embedded feeling that has been created by humankind is the nuclear bomb. These phenomena are all destroyers of embedded feeling, and are thus creators of scattered feeling.

Planets

When feelings of a particular quality cluster together in a distinct section of the Universal Feeling Body, then this collection of feelings will become increasingly deeply embedded. An obvious example of this clustering occurs in the segments of the Universe that humans call planets. What humans call planets, are, in the unobserved Universe, deeply embedded networks of feelings. Does this way of talking seem odd to you? What humans call the planet Mercury is an area of what humans call our Solar System, but in the Universal Feeling Body this area it isn't a distinct object with a boundary. This area contains things and bits of things; collections of nodes of feeling that move in particular ways. Furthermore, these movements can be sensed in a particular way through a structured visual sensing. A 'planet' is simply a part in a human perceiver's observed Universe which comes into being in the same manner as what humans call an 'airplane' flying through the sky, what humans call an 'apple', and what humans call a 'speeding cricket ball', a 'cricket', a 'cricket bat', a 'bat', a 'batsman', and 'Batman'. In these situations, the movements of networks of feelings are being visually sensed in a particular way and then conceptually moulded into parts such as a batsman, or a planet.

Compared to the number of feelings that exist in the segment of the Universe that humans call a planet, the number of feelings that either join or leave this collection is trivially small. Phenomena such as fires, storms, asteroid strikes, and earthquakes, can scatter feeling on a planet. However, these areas of the Universal Feeling Body remain unchanged as shining beacons, as networks of feelings of a particular quality that are extremely deeply embedded.

Water

Let us consider the phenomenon of water. The nature of water is to flow. To flow through rivers, streams, taps, pipes, and aquifers. To flow across the surface of the Earth, propelled by both the wind and the tidal movements initiated by our circling Moon. To flow through the ground, to enter the roots of plants and trees, to evaporate and transpire, to move through the atmosphere, to fall back to the surface as rain and snow, to flow into oceans and lakes.

Rather than being a scatterer of feelings, we can think of water as a continuous and powerful transporter of feeling across large swathes of the Earth. As the feeling that is water flows it is continuously absorbing tiny traces of the feeling that it flows through, whilst simultaneously leaving its feeling trace on the bits of the Universal Feeling Body that it flows through. These immense flows of ever-changing feeling are continuously occurring across the Earth – on its surface, in its interior, and in its atmosphere. When one's human body drinks water, it is drinking the tiny traces of feeling that these feelings have absorbed from their surroundings as they journeyed to one's lips.

Phantom limbs

Humans who have had a limb removed often report that they still become aware of feelings that appear to be located where the limb used to be. We can surely get a unique insight into this phenomenon when we consider the human body as a deeply embedded collection of nodes of feeling within the Universal Feeling Body – a participant in networks of things that far transcend the illusory boundary of the animal body. From this perspective, when a limb is removed from an animal body this limb will still be deeply embedded both with the rest of this body and with its speck of thought/awareness. In other words, there is a continuing dual deep embeddedness.

Of course, the bit of the animal body that the detached limb will be most highly embedded with is the location at which it used to be attached; a location which has turned into a stump. Due to the continuing deep dual embeddedness, the speck of thought/awareness will still become aware of the feeling states in the detached limb, and the detached limb will still be deeply embedded with the rest of the animal body. The former is direct awareness of the feelings of the detached limb; the latter is the radiation of feeling between the detached limb and the stump/body.

In this scenario, the bonds of embeddedness between nodes of feeling in the detached limb and the rest of the animal body will be deepest between the stump and the detached limb, due to these segments of the Universe participating in more things and the stump having the maximal spatial embeddedness with the detached limb. This explains why the feeling states in the detached limb can easily appear to be located where the limb used to be when it was attached to the rest of the body. The awareness that a speck of thought/awareness has of the feeling states in the removed limb will gradually fade, as spatial proximity increases, and as the passage of time inevitably flows. So, the dual deep embeddedness gradually fades. In saying this, I am assuming that the detached limb is spatially separated from the rest of the animal body. If a detached limb of a human body was put in a rucksack which was continuously worn by the human body, then the dual embeddedness would not gradually fade.

Solar radiation

We can now consider the phenomenon of solar radiation. Sunlight pours into the Earth's atmosphere and hits the Earth's surface, where some of it is absorbed and some of it bounces back off into the Earth's atmosphere; this flow of feeling then either interacts with feelings in the atmosphere, or escapes back into outer space. The flow of sunlight is a very powerful flow of feeling. Feelings are pouring into the Earth's atmosphere, pummelling the Earth's surface, and this barrage of feeling interacts with all of the feelings that it meets on its path. This includes the bodies of humans, the polar ice sheets, and the molecules in the atmosphere.

Radio waves and cables

Let us here consider the movement patterns of feelings that humans conceptually mould as Wi-Fi waves, other radio waves, Ethernet cables, and electricity cables. These phenomena are flows of feeling that can be thought of as being similar to water due to being continuous transporters of feeling across large swathes of the Earth. Continuous flows of feeling which modify the feelings that they flow through, whilst simultaneously being modified by the feelings that they flow through.

The feeling evolution of human culture

If we take a historical perspective, then we can fruitfully contemplate the journey that is the evolution of human culture as it has morphed from isolated communities, through the era of discovery/exploration, the Age of Imperialism, and into the increasingly globalised world of today. At the start of this journey of cultural evolution, feelings were relatively deeply embedded in distinct locations. The journey of human cultural evolution is a journey of increasing flows of feeling, and of increasing mixing of different qualities of feeling, across an increasingly large area. This increasing area initially encompasses almost exclusively the surface of the Earth, but as the journey of human cultural evolution progresses it increasingly extends out into the Earth's troposphere, and ultimately increasingly extends into outer space.

The globalised world of today

The globalised world of today is a frantic world of continuously flowing high-level feelings, and non-high-level feelings, across the surface of the Earth and through its atmosphere. The hallmarks of this frantic globalised world are the technological bringing forths which have enabled these continuous flows of feeling: the cars, the motorbikes, the trains, the boats, the airplanes, the helicopters, the spacecraft, the satellites, the submarines, the hand-gliders, the hovercraft, the tanks, the bridges, the tunnels, the skis, and the cable cars.

The epicentres of flowing feeling in the globalised world of today are its cities, with their high density populations, tall buildings, shopping malls, cafes, airports, dense flows of electricity / energy / radio waves, and their free-flowing webs of feeling that are precisely channelled through intricate transportation infrastructures.

The interactions of feelings

You know that the feelings within the Universal Feeling Body are divided into three categories: nodes of low-level feelings, medium-level feelings, and high-level feelings. When two low-level feelings interact the resulting feeling is a low-level feeling. In a similar fashion, when two medium-level feelings interact the resulting feeling is a medium-level feeling, and when two high-level feelings interact the resulting feeling is a high-level feeling. What happens when two feelings from different levels interact? When a low-level feeling interacts with a medium-level feeling, the resulting feeling is a medium-level feeling. When a low-level feeling interacts with a high-level feeling, the resulting feeling is a high-level feeling. And, when a medium-level feeling interacts with a high-level feeling, the resulting feeling is a high-level feeling.

The enlivening boost in feeling

We have explored how the unfolding of the Universal Feeling Body is directed towards the bringing forth of increasingly intense feelings. To talk of such directed evolution to increasingly intense feelings, is to talk of an unfolding journey from low-level feelings to medium-level feelings to high-level feelings. When higher level feelings come into existence they enliven their lower level feeling surroundings when they interact with them. For instance, when human bodies interact with low-level and medium-level feelings they enliven these bits of the Universal Feeling Body. Through such enlivening, the collection of nodes of high-level feeling that is a human body temporarily brings into being high-level feeling in that which can itself only originate either low-level feeling or medium-level feeling.

The enlivening boost in feeling is not something that is surprising, or mysterious. For, the Universal Feeling Body is comprised of nodes and things. So, a human body is a collection of nodes of high-level feeling which participates in things. Many of these things will encompass both nodes of high-level feeling in the human body, and nodes of low-level and medium-level feeling which are embedded with the human body. When high-level feelings originate in these things, they instantly radiate throughout these things, and thereby enliven the other feelings that participate in these things. Of course, if a human body is in a crowd of animal bodies, then it will be participating in deeply embedded things which contain an enormous number of nodes of high-level feeling, and the high-level feelings of all of the animal bodies in the crowd will be radiating through each other, and exuberantly enlivening each other.

The enlivening boost in feeling is powerful, but it is also only very short-lived. It might be helpful to envision a human body walking across a field. As it steps upon the grass, the medium-level feelings that are the grass are temporarily transformed into high-level feelings. The walking journey creates a forever changing trail of feeling intensity, as the high-level feelings that have been created gradually transform back to medium-level feelings as the human body walks further and further away from the temporarily enlivened feelings. If you are struggling to envision this it might be helpful to visualise a chemtrail as an analogy. As an airplane speedily moves through the sky a chemtrail is created, and as the airplane moves further and further away from a particular bit of the chemtrail, this bit gradually dissipates into its surroundings.

Walking on feelings

Let us further consider the phenomenon of walking. When your human body is walking you might want to reflect upon what it is walking on. It might be walking on a non-living segment of the Universe. If this is the case, then it will be walking on low-level feelings. This activity causes new feelings to come into being, but it won't be causing any entity to be 'in pain', or to suffer, due to the absence of specks of thought/awareness in the non-living. However, traces of feeling from what is being walked on will become absorbed into one's human body, and traces of the feeling in one's human body will become absorbed into the feelings that are being walked on.

Your human body could be walking on a segment of the Universe that is alive but lacking thought/awareness. In this case, it will be walking on medium-level feelings. A typical example would be walking on grass. This activity causes new feelings to come into being, but due to the absence of specks of thought/awareness in grass, your human body will not be causing the grass to be 'in pain', or to suffer, through the act of walking on it. However, traces of the feelings generated by the activity will be absorbed into both your human body and the grass.

Alternatively, your human body could be walking on a segment of the Universe that is alive and that is also very deeply embedded with a speck of thought/awareness. It could walk on another human, a cat, a dog, a fish, a horse, a cow, a rat, a mouse, a bird, a snake, or an insect. In this scenario, as one's human body is walking on nodes of high-level feeling that are very deeply embedded with a speck of thought/awareness, the feelings that are generated by this activity can very easily cause the speck of thought/awareness to be 'in pain' and to suffer. This activity will leave a feeling mark on both the body of the animal that is being walked on and the body of the animal that is doing the walking.

Jumping on grass

You have probably already realised that the account that has just been provided concerning walking on different levels of feeling is simplistic and requires elucidation. There are two reasons for this. Firstly, due to the instant radiation of feeling throughout things, and in particular the enlivening boost in feeling, there is a distinction between the level of feeling that a node can originate and the level of feeling that can exist in the node. Secondly, due to the fact that, at a particular moment in time, some nodes of medium-level and low-level feeling can be very deeply embedded with a speck of thought/awareness.

The combination of these two factors means that if one were to walk on nodes of low-level or medium-level feeling, then it is possible that the feelings thereby generated could enter the awareness of a speck of thought/awareness. And if these feelings had a quality which was extremely unpleasant, then the outcome could be that one had caused another speck, or even oneself, to be 'in pain' through the act of walking on grass, or walking on a pavement. There are three factors in play here: firstly, the embeddedness of low-level or medium-level nodes of feeling with a speck of thought/awareness; secondly, these nodes being subject to an enlivening boost in feeling into the realm of high-level feeling; thirdly, the quality of the feeling being extremely unpleasant.

Let us consider the possibility that one could cause another speck of thought/awareness to be 'in pain' through the activity that is one's human body jumping on grass. This effect is definitely not common or pronounced. For, the feelings within the Universal Feeling Body that enter the awareness of a speck of thought/awareness are typically high-level feelings. Furthermore, it is extremely unlikely that a speck of thought/awareness will be deeply embedded with the feelings that one's human body is jumping on. Yet, it will be fruitful for us to consider a plausible scenario. This scenario involves 'jumping' rather than 'walking' as this makes the scenario more vivid.

Envision that a human body is continuously lying on some grass for ten hours, whilst sunbathing. As we have explored, this interaction will temporarily enliven the grass and turn it into high-level feelings. Imagine that at the end of this ten hour period the human body gets up and walks away, and that another human body immediately walks onto the same piece of grass and starts jumping up and down on it. In this situation, it would not be surprising if the speck of thought/awareness of the human body who had been sunbathing for ten hours were to become aware of the feelings that were generated by the other human body jumping up and down on the grass. Furthermore, the quality of these feelings will be repulsive and unpleasant, so the speck of thought/awareness of the human body that had been sunbathing might become aware of a sense of unease, and might possibly even be 'in pain'. However, due to the widespread misattribution of feeling, the cause of this sense of unease, or the feelings of pain, are likely to be wrongly attributed as originating within the speck of thought/awareness's own human body.

The return of the spectacles, the toes, and the rabbit

You will recall that we earlier explored the relationship between a speck of thought/awareness and the nodes of feeling that it is embedded with by considering the collections of nodes of feeling that are spectacles, toes, and a rabbit. We concluded that a speck of thought/awareness could be more associated with a pair of spectacles than with the toes in its close travelling companion; yet, that this doesn't entail it being more likely that it will become more aware of the feelings in the spectacles than the feelings in the toes; for, the spectacles are nodes of low-level feeling.

Now that we have considered the enlivening boost in feeling, we can see that, in reality, the spectacles are actually going to be continuously in a state of enlivenment when they are on the head of an animal body. And, we can appreciate that such enlivenment greatly increases the likelihood that the speck of thought/awareness in the animal body will become aware of the feelings in the nodes of feeling that are the spectacles. Indeed, depending on the intensity of the feelings that exist at any moment in time, the speck of thought/awareness might be more likely to become aware of the feelings in the spectacles than it is the feelings in the rabbit. And, depending on the intensity of the feelings that exist at any moment in time, the speck of thought/awareness might be more likely to become aware of the feelings in the spectacles than the feelings in the toes, or it might be more likely to become aware of the feelings in the toes than the feelings in the spectacles.

The feeling associations of a tree

A tree is a conceptually moulded part that is a segment of the Universe. It is a collection of nodes of origination of medium-level feelings in the Universal Feeling Body. The feelings that are originated in this segment of the Universe are instantly radiated throughout the things in which the nodes of feeling participate. That which is visually perceived as a tree is, in the unobserved Universe, things, and bits of things.

The segment of the Universe that can potentially be visually sensed and conceptually moulded as a 'tree' has an immense plethora of forever changing spatial-temporal feeling associations with its surroundings, and within itself. Every one of these changes creates new things. As a squirrel approaches the tree and climbs its trunk and branches, it becomes more highly associated with the tree – feeling links between the squirrel and the tree become increasingly amplified. Memories are stored. Familiarity increases. The high-level feelings that are the squirrel temporarily enliven some of the medium-level feelings that are the tree. As a leaf becomes detached from the tree, and gets carried away from it by the wind, the feeling associations between the leaf and the tree very gradually weaken, as both spatial proximity increases and time passes. As water moves through the roots of a tree, and up through its trunk, feeling associations between water and roots/trunk are forged. The low-level feelings that are water are temporarily enlivened by the medium-level feelings that are the tree. As drops of water evaporate through the leaves of the tree the new feeling associations that have been forged remain as the drops continue their journey through the Earth's atmosphere. Of course, the feelings that are the raindrops leaving the tree will be forever changing as they continuously forge new spatial-temporal associations with their surroundings – the other feelings in the Universal Feeling Body.

 # Human concepts are collections of nodes of a particular level of feeling; and, these concepts might, or might not, correspond to a concrete difference in the Universal Feeling Body

You should be starting to come to know the forever changing nexus of feeling associations within the Universal Feeling Body. Pick any object (any concept that you have, which has resulted in you having a moulded part in your observed Universe). You will have a label to refer to this object, whether it is 'sauce', 'sage', or 'sausage'; whether it is 'rain', 'bow', or 'rainbow'. This object/label points to something that you have conceptually moulded; it points to a boundaried entity that you have boundaried, have created, in the process of making sense of your visual sensings. These labelled objects, these parts, these arbitrary entities, are concepts.

Let us consider objects/labels/parts/concepts such as a 'bench', a 'chair', a 'flower', a 'ladder', a 'cup', a 'sausage', a 'seagull', and a 'book'. Such objects are parts in my observed Universe, and I imagine that they are also parts in your observed Universe. As we have already started to explore, these moulded parts might, or they might not, correspond to actual concrete differences in the Universal Feeling Body.

Whether there is such a correspondence depends solely on the location of the part – what the part is surrounded by. For, the parts that we are considering – a 'bench', a 'chair', a 'flower', a 'ladder', a 'cup', a 'sausage', a 'seagull', and a 'book' – are each collections of nodes of a particular level of feeling. They are either collections of nodes of low-level feeling, medium-level feeling, or high-level feeling. If the moulded part / collection of nodes is surrounded by nodes of a different level of feeling, then the moulded part will correspond to an actual concrete difference in this portion of the Universal Feeling Body.

Let us consider an example. One of my concepts/parts is a 'chair'. This chair is a collection of nodes of low-level feeling. If it is one of thousands of chairs in an empty football stadium, then it will be surrounded by, engulfed by, an immense plethora of other nodes of low-level feeling. In this scenario, my concept/moulding of a 'chair' does not correspond to a concrete difference in this portion of the Universal Feeling Body. However, if this segment of the Universe – what I call a 'chair' – is removed from the football stadium and placed in a tropical rainforest, then it will be a collection of nodes of low-level feeling that is surrounded by nodes of medium-level feeling. In this case, my concept/moulding of a 'chair' corresponds to a concrete difference in the Universal Feeling Body.

Analogous scenarios can be described for the rest of my concepts that we are considering here. For instance, the part/concept in my observed Universe that I call a 'seagull' is a collection of nodes of high-level feeling. If this seagull is standing on top of a concrete building, by itself, then it is a collection of nodes of high-level feeling that is surrounded by nodes of low-level feeling, and my concept/moulding will thus correspond to a concrete difference in the Universal Feeling Body. However, if the seagull is joined on the roof by hundreds of other seagulls, and if these seagulls form a jam-packed colony, with their bodies all jostling up tightly against each other, then there exists an immense mass of nodes of high-level feeling. And, consequently, my 'seagull' concept/moulding will no longer correspond to a concrete difference in this portion of the Universal Feeling Body.

We have here been considering simple concepts/mouldings – particular objects/parts that I visually perceive in my immediate surroundings. These simple concepts are all collections of nodes of a particular level of feeling. If we switch our attention to complex concepts, then it need not be the case that these concepts are nodes of a particular level of feeling. For instance, I have the complex concept of 'the planet Earth'; and, this concept contains all three of the levels of feeling. Yet, this is more of an abstract concept that I have developed within myself, within the speck of thought/awareness that is me. For, it is not something that I have ever visually sensed and conceptually moulded into a part in my observed Universe. However, if I had been an astronaut, then 'the planet Earth', with its three levels of feeling, would actually be a visually sensed and conceptually moulded part in my observed Universe.

The overwhelming majority of my concepts, and your concepts, are collections of nodes of a particular level of feeling.

The feeling associations of the Universal Feeling Body

If you envision one particular part in your observed Universe – a 'cup', perhaps – then you can attempt to behold the forever changing nature of the spatial-temporal feeling associations that exist in the things that are this segment of the Universe. After one has achieved this, one can then envision not just the changing feeling associations of one particular part; one can attempt to behold the entire Universal Feeling Body as a singular borderless entity. Envision feelings moving at a vast range of different speeds. Envision a rich mosaic of continuously changing feelings. Envision networks of feelings overlaying, overlapping and underlaying networks of feelings. Envision feelings co-radiating throughout their things. Envision some things becoming larger by acquiring nodes of feeling, whilst other things inevitably become smaller as some of their constituent nodes of feeling become segregated due to spatial-temporal separation. Envision nodes of feeling from higher levels enlivening lower level nodes.

As the planet spins on its axis, as the Earth moves around the Sun, as the Moon moves around the Earth, as the oceans move across the surface of the Earth, as the fish swim through the oceans, as the birds fly through the sky, as the worms burrow through the earth, as the humans pile onto carriages on the London Underground, as airplanes glide through the sky, as clouds drift through the sky, as the glaciers melt, as the canary sings, as the cue hits the ball, and as the grandfather clock strikes midnight, an immense plethora of feeling associations are both forged and loosened. Continuously emerging feelings instantly co-radiate through a ginormous number of ever-changing things; networks of feelings are overlapping and underlaying countless other networks of feelings.

Becoming overwhelmed by feeling – density and quality of feeling

We have considered the stark division within the Universal Feeling Body between sites of deeply embedded feeling and sites of scattered feeling. It should be noted that an animal body can become overwhelmed by being in a site of deeply embedded feeling. That is to say, the particular density of feeling, quality of feeling, and pervasiveness of feeling, that is present in a particular location can overwhelm, can overpower and dominate, the pre-existing feelings in an animal body. If one were to find oneself in this situation, then one could boost one's wellbeing by spending some time in a site of scattered feeling, where the lack of embeddedness prevents one from being overwhelmed in this way. An example of this would be becoming overwhelmed in a city centre and rejuvenating oneself by spending time at the seaside on the beach.

It is also possible that the opposite might be true. It might be the case that a human body is 'all at sea' / 'all over the place' in a site of scattered feeling. In this case, it would be advantageous for the human body to go to a site of deeply embedded feeling that is known to have a quality of feeling that is beneficial. For example, a human body might literally be 'all at sea' on the sea, and become rejuvenated by relocating to a meditation centre, or ancient woodland, or a library.

Becoming overwhelmed by feeling – levels of feeling

An animal body can also become overwhelmed by feeling when it is in a location which is dominated by a particular level of feeling / a particular mode of the Universe. This is a phenomenon that you are surely very familiar with. Recall that there are three different levels of feeling within the Universal Feeling Body: low-level feeling, medium-level feeling, and high-level feeling. There are likely to be times when you have been in a location that is dominated by one of these levels of feeling, and you have known that your human body is ill at ease and needs to be moved to a very different type of location.

Locations of low-level feeling are places that are dominated by the non-living segments of the Universe. For instance, such locations could be one's home, or an abandoned industrial estate, or a desert.

Locations of medium-level feeling are places that are dominated by the segments of the Universe that are living without thought/awareness. For instance, such locations could be a forest, a park, or a garden.

Locations of high-level feeling are places that are dominated by the segments of the Universe that are living with thought/awareness. For instance, such locations could be a busy gymnasium, a busy café, a busy pub, an abattoir, or a busy shopping mall.

If you become aware that your human body is ill at ease in a particular location, then you will almost instinctively recognise what level of feeling that you are surrounded by, and you will realise that you need to move to a location which has a different level of feeling. So, if you are in a busy shopping mall, you might realise that you need to move to a park, or to go home. And, if you are at home, you might realise that you need to go to a garden, or a forest, or a place where there are lots of human bodies.

Becoming overwhelmed by thought – negative thought spirals

The feeling state of an animal body, and the wellbeing of an animal body, is determined by its feeling surroundings – both the level of feeling in the surroundings, and the density and quality of this feeling. There is another issue which needs to be addressed. This is the issue of how a speck of thought/awareness thinks about the feeling state of its animal body, and how it thinks about the life of its animal body in general. Thought processes can go one of two ways. They can be of an optimistic 'glass half full' variety, or they can be of a pessimistic 'glass half empty' variety. In this way, thought processes tend to spiral in a particular direction, and this direction affects the wellbeing of the animal body in which the speck of thought/awareness is located. For, negative thought spirals lead to suboptimal decisions/actions, and thereby to bodily feelings of repulsion.

We previously considered the development of negative thought spirals in the context of a speck of thought/awareness being prohibited from actualising the potentials of its animal body. This prohibition arose from sources outside the control of the speck; for instance, we considered a bird that was locked inside a cage. In situations such as these, it is exceptionally hard for a speck of thought/awareness to avoid negative thought spirals. These situations are a subset of the range of situations in which negative thought spirals can develop; negative thought spirals typically arise in the absence of prohibition from outside sources.

Becoming overwhelmed – conclusion: there are no islands

The wellbeing of an animal body is affected by the feelings that it is engulfed by – both the level of these feelings, and the density and quality of these feelings – and by the pessimistic or optimistic thought spirals of its speck of thought/awareness.

The wellbeing of a human body, its feeling state, is determined by the feelings that it is engulfed by. No segment is an island. No moulded part is an island. No feeling is an island. No speck is an island. And, no thing is an island.

The senses of the human body

You are a speck of thought/awareness that is situated within two bodies – a human body in your observed Universe, and a Universal Feeling Body in the unobserved Universe. The Universal Feeling Body is constituted by nodes of feeling: low-level feelings, medium-level feelings, and high-level feelings. It is time for us to consider the question: How do these feelings relate to the senses of the human body? The short answer to this question is: the senses of the human body are either simply the Universal Feeling Body – feelings feeling feelings, or they are a moulding of the Universal Feeling Body. There is, of course, much more to be said.

Tastes = smells = sounds = bodily sensations = touches = feelings

When an 'I', a speck of thought/awareness, becomes aware that its animal body has feelings of 'pain', has 'pins and needles', is touching something that is 'ice-cold', is smelling something 'putrid', is tasting something 'bitter', and is hearing a 'spine-tingling scream', then it is becoming aware of the feelings of its Universal Feeling Body. Feelings have a quality that can be pointed to through words such as 'fragrant', 'taste', 'smell', 'bodily sensation', 'sweetness', 'musty', 'rank', 'aching', 'pain', 'spicy', 'tingling', 'nauseating', 'jarring', 'foul', 'hot', 'cacophony', 'melodious', 'crackling', 'pungent', 'dissonance', 'exhilarating', 'pleasant', 'din', and 'putrid'. Such feelings pervade, and constitute, the Universal

Feeling Body. When a speck of thought/awareness becomes aware that its human body has a bodily sensation, or becomes aware that its human body hears something, tastes something, smells something, or has the sensation of touching something, then it is really just becoming aware of the feelings of its Universal Feeling Body.

The idea that there is a difference between tastes, smells, sounds, bodily sensations, and the feelings of touch, arises due to the incessant need of a speck of thought/awareness to create boundaries/divisions in that which is boundaryless. To talk of there being 'five human senses' only makes sense in the observed Universe of parts. From the perspective of the Universal Feeling Body, the deeper reality of what is occurring can be appreciated. What humans call a sound is a feeling. What humans call a taste is a feeling. What humans call a smell is a feeling. What humans call the quality of touching something is a feeling. What humans call a bodily sensation is a feeling. Feelings are feelings; in the Universal Feeling Body there are not divisions between types of feelings. These feelings constitute the continuously moving and radiating flow of feeling that is the Universal Feeling Body. Such feelings pervade the Universe.

A melodious/spicy/aching/musty feeling

When feelings feel each other in a particular bit of the Universal Feeling Body, and thereby become themselves, then in terms of human labels, human concepts, this feeling interaction might quite aptly be described as a 'melodious/spicy/aching/musty' feeling. There is just one type of feeling – feeling is feeling. Yet, in the observed Universe feeling can be conceptually carved up and labelled as 'sound', as 'taste', and so on. In the unobserved Universe there are just interactions between feelings – feelings feeling feelings – which creates diverse movement patterns; whilst, in the observed Universe parts are conceptually moulded and labelled, parts such as: ears, tongues, noses, and skin.

To say that there is a feeling in one's nose, and a feeling in one's mouth, is the same kind of assertion as saying that there is a feeling in one's finger and a feeling in one's toe. And, such feelings also exist throughout the Universal Feeling Body, in what one conceptually moulds as, say, stones, scones, thrones, bones, and drones.

Music

Music is a state of feeling, a very powerful state of feeling. It is also a very quickly moving feeling, and this speed contributes to its power. Every sound, every note, every chord, is simultaneously a state of vibration and a state of feeling; a state that surges through the Universal Feeling Body. It surges, and as it surges it also radiates. This surging cascade of feeling changes the feeling of all that it encounters, whilst itself being subtly modified by the feelings that it encounters as it surges.

There is an immense diversity of musical styles. That is to say, there are feelings of very different qualities and patterns. When these qualities and patterns surge through your two bodies – your human body, and your Universal Feeling Body – the feeling states of these two bodies will be significantly changed. You might become aware of stimulating, blissful, invigorating, uplifting, euphoric feelings; or, you might become aware of jarring, unpleasant, uncomfortable feelings. The type of feelings that come into existence will be determined by whether or not the feelings of your human body chime with the qualities and patterns of the musical feelings. Harmonious chiming entails uplifting feelings; a lack of such chiming entails jarring feelings.

The feeling of speech is divorced from its linguistic content

Human speech is a state of feeling. When a human body speaks it is creating feeling. That is to say, it is originating flows of feeling which project out from their point of origin, in a similar manner to the way that music surges through the Universal Feeling Body. The vocally created feelings also radiate throughout the things that the originating feeling participates in. As the vocally created feeling powerfully surges through the Universal Feeling Body it encounters new things, and it consequently also radiates throughout these things.

The state of feeling that is vocally created is divorced from the linguistic content of the uttered words. The same string of words can be uttered with very different feeling. The feeling of this string of words can be harmonious and concordant, or it can be jarring and dissonant. The feeling of this string of words can be pleasant/loving/supportive, or it can be unpleasant/aggressive/menacing.

The auditory sense – the awareness of the feelings of one's Universal Feeling Body

The auditory sense in one's human body – one's ears – senses some of the feelings in one's Universal Feeling Body. For, what one's ears can hear partially constitutes one's Universal Feeling Body. One's ears are feeling structures that are structured so as to sense a certain range of the feelings that exist in one's Universal Feeling Body. The linguistic contents of uttered words that we encountered in the previous section do not exist in the Universal Feeling Body; what exists, and what is auditorily sensed, are solely movement patterns of feelings.

Following an auditory sensing, a speck of thought/awareness typically attempts to make sense of the feelings that have been sensed. These feelings could be interpreted as, say: 'a bird chirping', 'waves hitting the shore', 'a linguistic utterance', and so on. The endeavour to interpret, to make sense of, the significance of the feelings that have been sensed is an endeavour that is the sole domain of a speck of thought/awareness. When a particular type of auditorily sensed feeling has been categorised by a speck as, say: 'a bird chirping', then computation processes in the brain can readily re-identify this categorisation when the same feeling is auditorily sensed in the future; there is no need to make sense of the feeling. However, in the absence of a categorisation by a speck, there are just uncategorised feelings. Such interpretation and categorisation is a very different endeavour from the phenomenon of an animal body being exposed to, and interacting with, the feeling content of auditorily sensed feelings. For, these feelings interact with the feelings that are the entire animal body.

The categorisation of auditorily sensed feelings by a speck arises from an interpretation of certain feelings in the Universal Feeling Body. This interpretation/categorisation is a translation of feelings into what we can call non-feeling outputs / auditory outputs. These outputs are distinct from the feelings in which they are instantiated. These outputs are the categorisations of a speck of thought/awareness. Auditory outputs might be a string of words that have been interpreted, for instance: *'Shall we go to Reed Hall or to The Forum'*, or they could simply point at the hypothesised cause of the feeling, for instance: 'dog barking', 'flask top being screwed', 'car approaching', or 'human screaming'.

When auditorily sensed feeling has been translated by a speck into an auditory output, it can then synthesise this output with the feeling content in order to make a decision concerning whether, and how, its human body needs to act/respond. This is particularly important when the auditory output is a linguistic utterance.

 # The sense of smell – the awareness of the feelings of one's Universal Feeling Body

When the speck of thought/awareness in a human body becomes aware of a feeling that is located in the nose of its human body, it often uses the word 'smell' to refer to this feeling.

When feelings enter the nose, the feelings in the nose and the way that they are structured/moving determines which new feelings come into being. In other words, the feelings that come into being are a fusion of the feeling that enters the nose and the feeling structure of the nose itself.

The sense of taste – the awareness of the feelings of one's Universal Feeling Body

When the speck of thought/awareness in a human body becomes aware of a feeling that is located on the tongue of its human body, whilst ingesting, it typically uses the word 'taste' to refer to this feeling.

When feelings enter the mouth, the feelings in the mouth and the way that they are structured/moving determines which new feelings come into being. In other words, the feelings that come into being are a fusion of the feeling that enters the mouth and the feeling structure of the mouth itself.

The sense of touch – the awareness of the feelings of one's Universal Feeling Body

When the speck of thought/awareness in a human body becomes aware of a feeling that is located where its human body makes contact with its surroundings, it typically uses the phrase 'sense of touch' to refer to this feeling.

When these feelings arise they are a fusion of the feelings in the bit of the human body that is making contact with its surroundings, and the feelings that exist in the bit of the surroundings that contact is being made with.

Bodily sensations – the awareness of the feelings of one's human body

When the speck of thought/awareness in a human body becomes aware of a feeling that is located inside its human body, it typically uses the phrase 'bodily sensation' to refer to this feeling.

These feelings, like all feelings, arise due to the movements of nodes of feeling. These feelings can be caused by movements within the human body itself, or by movements outside the human body, in the things that the human body participates in.

The labelling of feelings

When the speck of thought/awareness in a human body becomes aware of a feeling it typically attaches a label to the feeling. For instance: 'a rancid stench', 'a sweet taste', 'an ache in my left thigh', 'a jarring cacophony', 'a motorbike', 'a bird chirping', 'a toothache', 'a song', 'a rough texture', 'a pleasant aroma', and 'a prickly sensation'. Such labelling is arbitrary; it merely points towards the fact that a speck of thought/awareness has become aware of a feeling in its Universal Feeling Body.

When these labels are created they either explicitly or implicitly point towards the hypothesised cause of the feeling. A label can be attached to either the feeling itself, or to its hypothesised cause. So, the label 'a rancid stench' could easily be replaced by: 'someone has broken wind'. Both of these labels are valid. You might recall that when we explored auditorily sensed feelings, that we considered the difference between the feeling that is auditorily sensed and the auditory output that is created when this feeling is interpreted and categorised by a speck of thought/awareness. We are now taking this distinction a stage further by considering all of the feelings that a speck of thought/awareness becomes aware of, and making three distinctions: firstly, the existence of a feeling in its uninterpreted/unlabelled state; secondly, the attempt to describe this feeling through labelling it; thirdly, the fact that this label either implicitly or explicitly points at the hypothesised cause of the feeling. So, the labels 'a sweet taste' and 'blueberry' both point at: 'the blueberries that are in the mouth'. Whilst, the labels 'grating jarring roaring vroom' and 'motor engine' both point at: 'the motorbike that is cruising along the road'. This feeling could also be labelled as: 'a motorbike'.

 # The visual sense – visual perception is visual sensing and conceptual moulding

In the previous several sections we have been considering how a speck of thought/awareness becomes aware of some of the feelings in its Universal Feeling Body via its animal body. Most animal bodies also have a visual sense. The visual sense is very different; for, it is not grounded in the realm of feeling. It is not a detector of feeling. It is not feeling feeling feeling. All of the other senses that we have just considered are interactions of feelings in the Universal Feeling Body; feeling interactions which can be interpreted and labelled. The visual sense is very different; it just senses movement in the Universal Feeling Body. In other words, its realm is the observed Universe.

As we have already explored, the movement patterns that are visually sensed are determined by the structure of the visual sense and how medium-grained it is. When movements are visually sensed, a speck of thought/awareness seeks to impose order, to identify common patterns, and this results in the conceptual moulding of that which is visually sensed into distinct parts/objects. In this way, boundaries are created, brought into being, and the Universal Feeling Body gets transformed into a particular observed Universe – an appearance that contains particular divisions. Visual perception has two distinct components: visual sensing of movement and apparent non-movement, and conceptual moulding.

A speck requires divisions and separations, artificial boundaries, if it is to make sense of its surroundings and thereby successfully navigate its animal body through its surroundings. Such boundaries are required in order to survive: to identify food, to procreate, to find shelter, and to avoid danger. Through visual perception a speck perceives colours and shapes; these phenomena are delineators; markers of boundaries. The visual sense possessed by animals can be constructed in a multitude of different ways, with each unique construction latching on to different movement patterns. Furthermore, the particular movement patterns that are visually sensed, along with apparent non-movement, can be conceptually moulded in a plethora of different ways. All of this means that there are an immense array of possible observed Universes.

Where one speck visually perceives a great number of parts, each with a different colour, another speck can visually perceive just one singularly-coloured part. We are here talking about one discreet segment of the Universe. One speck visually perceives lots of objects and colours in this segment of the Universe. Another speck visually perceives just one object and one colour in this segment of the Universe. Human visual perception entails the creation of an immense plethora of divisions.

Visual perception is a structured sensing and conceptual moulding of the movements that are created by the interactions of feelings.

The moulded Universe versus the unmoulded Universe

The visual sense is extremely powerful, but it is also highly superficial. Its sensings are structured, and it provides the structure. That which is visually sensed is an intricately constructed kaleidoscope of differential movement, and apparent non-movement of that which is moving. The particular movement patterns that are sensed, and the accompanying mirage of non-movement, is determined by the structure of the visual sense. These visual sensings are moulded by a speck into parts, distinct objects, boundaried entities, concepts. The visually observed Universe is a moulded Universe; it is not reality in its unmoulded state.

The unmoulded Universe, the Universe in its unobserved state, is, of course, the intermingling differentially-embedded matrix of feelings that is the Universal Feeling Body. It is the 'one giant movement pattern' that is the Universal Moving Body. A speck has direct unmediated access to the unmoulded Universe via the things that its animal body participates in. These things are networks of nodes of feeling in which the nodes of feeling that constitute an animal body are typically tiny components. It is these nodes of feeling that the speck of thought/awareness in a human body is becoming aware of when it asserts that it has a bodily sensation, that it has smelt something, that it has tasted something, that it is in pain, that it has heard something, or that it has had the sensation of touching something.

The awareness of sounds=feelings

It will be fruitful for us to explore a little further here the nature of the sounds=feelings that a speck of thought/awareness might become aware of. A speck of thought/awareness might become aware of feelings which it categorises as: 'the rustling of leaves', 'instrumental music', 'birds chirping', 'cat meowing', 'dog barking', 'car breaks squeaking', 'helicopter blades rotating', 'the clickety-clack of a train', 'clock ticking', 'the howling in pain of a human', 'unintelligible gibberish', and 'linguistic utterances' (for instance: 'Shall we go for a walk from Causeland Railway Station to St Keyne Wishing Well'). These are all auditory outputs.

In all of these situations, a speck of thought/awareness is becoming aware of the feelings that exist in its Universal Feeling Body, and it is then attributing significance to these feelings. There is no moulding of the Universal Feeling Body. There is just direct awareness of feelings. Yet, this awareness is partial; for, ears are structured so as to only enable access to a certain range of the feelings that exist in the Universal Feeling Body.

The synthesis of the moulding of parts in visual perception and the categorisation of feeling in auditory sensing

We have just explored how auditory sensing entails the direct awareness of feelings, and we have considered how these sensed feelings come to be categorised by a speck of thought/awareness as auditory outputs. This categorisation inevitably points to the hypothesised source of the feeling; so, a feeling could be taken to emanate from, say: 'a cat meowing'.

The feeling that is categorised as 'a cat meowing' could conceivably be categorised as such in the absence of visual perception. However, in practice, one's categorisation of auditorily sensed feelings – such as: 'a cat meowing' – is typically bound up with visual perception. For, when a speck of thought/awareness categorises a particular type of feeling as 'a cat meowing' it arrives at this particular categorisation due to associating it with the part in its observed Universe that it has conceptually moulded as 'a cat'.

Mouldings of the Universal Feeling Body versus awareness of the Universal Feeling Body

Visual perception is a moulding of that which feels: the Universal Feeling Body. Whereas, the auditory sense, the sense of smell, the sense of touch, the sense of taste, and bodily sensations, are all points of access into the Universal Feeling Body itself. These points of access enable a speck of thought/awareness to become aware of its Universal Feeling Body.

The currantless bun versus an unobservable division

Let us explore a little further the nature of the relationship between the Universal Feeling Body and a speck of thought/awareness. The Universal Feeling Body is a singular entity which has no divisions within it when specks do not exist. What does this statement mean? It means that if no specks of thought/awareness exist in the Universal Feeling Body, then it is a boundaryless singular entity. The Universe is a boundaryless singular entity. Whereas, if a speck of thought/awareness exists, then there can be said to be a division in the Universal Feeling Body.

We earlier imagined that the Universe is a currant bun. In the absence of any specks of thought/awareness, all that exists is a currantless bun. If a speck of thought/awareness exists, then there is a currant in the bun. A speck of thought/awareness brings into being a division in the Universal Feeling Body. Yet, this is not a division that is observable. One cannot observe currants in the bun, even if there are millions of them.

As specks are *unobservable* divisions, when these divisions exist it can still sensibly be said that the Universe is a boundaryless singular entity. This can sensibly be said from the perspective of the observed Universe; for, from this vantage point, there are no boundaries/objects/parts that are simultaneously potentially observable, and that have an existence that is independent of an observation. All that exists independently, as a divided entity, is the unobservable creator of boundaries, the moulder of parts. If there are currants in the bun, then unobservable divisions exist.

Specks of thought/awareness are brought forth into existence due to the unfolding evolution of the Universal Feeling Body. The bringing forth of the first speck within the Universal Feeling Body was the bringing forth of the first division in the Universe. Why is this the case? Through this bringing forth the Universe became aware of itself, and pondered itself; and, such awareness entails that the Universe inevitably saw itself as a divided entity – the 'I' and the 'not-I': the speck and the parts.

Science

Science enables humans to increasingly get to know the movements of the parts in their observed Universe. That is to say, science enables humans to increasingly get to know their conceptual mouldings of their structured visual sensings.

Physics and chemistry

Observed regularities in the interactions of conceptually moulded parts are repetitions of particular feeling attractions and feeling repulsions.

Ethics

Ethics is grounded in feeling. If a speck of thought/awareness initiates behaviour that intentionally brings into being feelings of repulsion for another speck then it is engaging in unethical behaviour. If you verbally insult a speck of thought/awareness, physically attack the animal body of a speck of thought/awareness, steal the possessions of a speck of thought/awareness, or intentionally bring into being any other kind of physical or mental suffering for a speck of thought/awareness, then you are intentionally bringing into being feelings of repulsion for that speck.

Coming from the opposite direction, ethical behaviour is behaviour that intentionally brings into being feelings of attraction for another speck of thought/awareness. Yet, if such behaviour simultaneously brings into being feelings of repulsion for a different speck of thought/awareness, then the behaviour might not be ethical. In this situation, one might want to compare the magnitudes involved: Are the feelings of attraction that are generated greater than the feelings of repulsion? Or, one might simply want to assert that the generation of any feelings of repulsion entails unethical behaviour. Alternatively, one might adopt the approach of 'listening to one's heart' and behave in the way that seems to one to be the most appropriate.

Unethical behaviour can justify unethical behaviour. So, if an animal body engages in extremely unethical behaviour, then the incarceration of that animal body is justified. The imprisonment would be unethical behaviour, in terms of it intentionally bringing into being feelings of repulsion in the speck of thought/awareness of the incarcerated; however, in this case engaging in unethical behaviour is justified. Indeed, such justification could be said to transform unethical behaviour into ethical behaviour.

Movement patterns, feelings, and abilities/skills/aptitudes

The Universal Feeling Body is a collection of different feelings, and the interactions of these feelings gives rise to different movement patterns. One can approach movement patterns from a different perspective, and thereby come to know the Universal Feeling Body as a collection of different abilities/skills/aptitudes. To say this is to say that every segment of the Universe has the potential to do something; and, when a segment actualises this potential, then a particular movement pattern comes into being. So, when one's human body visually senses a movement pattern, then it is sensing the actualisation of abilities/skills/aptitudes.

It is very important to realise that, due to the structured nature of visual sensing, there is a stark distinction between the movement patterns that are visually sensed and the movement that exists in the unobserved Universe. One way to get a handle on this distinction is to envision that there are no movement patterns in the unobserved Universe – there is just one moving whole; whereas, when one's visual sense visually senses a bit of this moving whole it isolates, even forges, particular patterns within the whole. Nevertheless, if we envision a particular bit of the unobserved Universe, it is clearly moving in a particular way independent of observation; so, this means that it can meaningfully be asserted that there are diverse movement patterns within the moving whole in the unobserved Universe.

Some bits of the Universal Feeling Body – animal bodies – contain specks of thought/awareness, whose task it is to enable these bits to flourish through enabling them to fully utilise their abilities/skills/aptitudes. The accomplishment of this task brings into being unique movement patterns and their associated unique feelings – high intensity feelings.

Personal identity

The phrase 'personal identity' is perhaps not that useful; for, the notion of a 'person' is not that useful; and, the notion of 'identity' is also not that useful! If one makes use of the notion of a 'person', then one probably has in mind a speck of thought/awareness. For, a speck of thought/awareness is that which is an 'I', and an 'I' is surely what one has in mind if one utilises the notion of a person. A speck of thought/awareness has an intermittent existence; it pops into existence and pops out of existence. Yet, there is continuity here; for, it pops into existence in the same animal body as it popped out of existence. A speck of thought/awareness is a qualityless window; yet, it still has a unique nature; for, 'thought/awareness leads to thought/awareness'. For instance, there can be negative thought spirals in some specks of thought/awareness, and positive thought spirals in other specks of thought/awareness.

There is a different way to think about the notion of a person. Every segment of the Universe has unique abilities/skills/aptitudes, which are grounded in 'personality'/'passions'. This means that when a segment of the Universe is moulded into a human body by a speck, that this human body will inevitably be a unique collection of abilities/skills/aptitudes, which are grounded in 'personality'/'passions'. This unique collection typically exists continuously in a human body throughout its existence –

from cradle to grave. However, the vigour with which this unique collection can be actualised inevitably varies through time. The typical adult has more vigour than a toddler, and the human body has less vigour as it becomes old and increasingly elderly. Perhaps the unique collection of these attributes that is instantiated in a particular human body might be what one has in mind, if one has the notion of a 'person'.

However, the most plausible notion of a 'person' is surely a combination of the above two possibilities. In other words, a 'person' should best be thought of as a speck of thought/awareness in combination with its close travelling companion – the unique collection of abilities/skills/aptitudes that are grounded in 'personality'/'passions', and which are located in the segment of the Universe that is the animal body. For, without this combination, the notion of a 'person' seems rather lacking, even squalid.

It is possible that one might find this proposed notion of a 'person' to be too broad. For, one might not be happy to assert that what one conceptually moulds as 'a pig' is a person, that what one conceptually moulds as 'a cow' is a person, that what one conceptually moulds as 'a cat' is a person, and that what one conceptually moulds as 'a herring' is a person. It would not be surprising if one was not happy to make these assertions; after all, the notion of a 'person' is a red herring, and thus the notion of 'personal identity' is also a red herring. Yet, it is also possible that one might be happy to assert that 'a herring' is a 'person'.

Beauty

Anything that is forged, created, by feelings of attraction is observable as beautiful. Yet, the troubled soul who is drowning in negative thought spirals, and not actualising their potential, will be blind to the beautiful.

Recap

Specks of thought/awareness emerge within the brains of animals. In one sense, the animal body – for example, the head, torso, arms, and legs, of a human body – can be said to be the body of a speck of thought/awareness. Such an assertion makes sense in the boundaried realm of the observed Universe. However, at a more fundamental level specks of thought/awareness emerge within the Universal Feeling Body, and, with the exception of the specks of thought/awareness themselves, the Universal Feeling Body is boundaryless – with all boundaries, all divisions, all distinct objects in an observed Universe, being the creations of a particular act of visual sensing and conceptual moulding. So, the real body, the ultimate body, of a speck of thought/awareness, is its Universal Feeling Body. And, every speck has a unique Universal Feeling Body.

The existence of a speck of thought/awareness within the Universal Feeling Body, the creation of an opposition, is the creation of an 'I'. A speck has an intermittent existence within an animal body; when it does not exist, then an 'I' does not exist. It is crucial to appreciate that a speck of thought/awareness is a qualityless window which is devoid of feeling, but which becomes directly aware of the feelings in its Universal Feeling Body (tastes = smells = sounds = bodily sensations = feelings). A speck takes, beholds, ponders, considers, the structured visual sensings that it is presented with and conceptually moulds them; this is an activity which brings into being its observed Universe of parts. These visual sensings are structured medium-grained sensings of the movements of the Universal Feeling Body. These movements themselves come into existence through the interactions of feelings – feelings feeling feelings – which results in feelings and their things actualising their abilities/skills/aptitudes. The feelings that exist in a particular bit of the Universal Feeling Body can be said to have 'personality'/'passions'. When a particular segment of the Universe moves in accordance with its 'personality'/'passions' then particular abilities/skills/aptitudes are actualised.

The Universal Feeling Body of a speck of thought/awareness is much larger than its animal body. A speck of thought/awareness frequently becomes aware of feelings that originate outside of, and exist outside of, its animal body; these are feelings that both originate in, and exist in, its Universal Feeling Body; for, a speck of thought/awareness cannot become aware of feelings that exist outside of its Universal Feeling Body. A speck of thought/awareness also becomes aware feelings that exist in its animal body but that originated outside of its animal body, due to the instant radiation of feeling throughout its Universal Feeling Body. However, due to the widespread misattribution of feeling, such feelings are typically assumed to have originated within its animal body.

The world of pure feeling

Can any sense be made of the idea that every feeling creates a 'world'; that it is somehow opposed to its surroundings? What about the things that are forged out of bonds between feelings? Can any sense be made of the idea that every thing creates a world? In short: Do feelings and/or things construct their surroundings in some way?

Let us recall that a 'thing' is a collection of bonded feelings, a network of feelings that are equally embedded within the Universal Feeling Body. The nodes of feeling that constitute a thing are continuously instantly radiating feeling throughout the thing. This continuous co-radiation of feeling means that at any moment in time a thing is permeated by a single feeling. Things are continuously changing in size – gaining nodes of feeling and loosing nodes of feeling – and they are also continuously changing in terms of their qualitative/feeling nature. Networks of feelings overlay, underlay, and overlap, networks of feelings, and every moment every network transforms into a slightly different thing. So, the part of my observed Universe that I conceptually mould as a 'tree' will contain an immense plethora of things, and bits of the 'tree' will also partially constitute an immense plethora of things. Things do not respect the boundary that I mould as the edges of a tree. Some things are tiny, and some things are massive.

Every feeling participates in things. No feeling is an island. Things interact with their surroundings by feeling the nodes of feeling of other things. This feeling of feelings – feeling feeling feeling interactions – is characterised by feelings of attraction and feelings of repulsion, and the qualitative content is that which a human might refer to as the feeling of tastes, smells, bodily sensations, sounds, and touches. The feeling of the nodes of feeling of the things that surround a thing is a continuous process that permeates the entire Universal Feeling Body. Furthermore, the nodes of feeling in a thing themselves feel, equally feel, all of the other nodes of feeling in the thing. This means that all things, and all nodes of feeling, have some kind of notion of their surroundings.

All things feel the nodes of feeling of other things. All feelings feel the other nodes of feeling in their things. Furthermore, nodes of feeling and things have memories of their previous feelings. As all feelings and things differentially feel that which is not themselves – feel that which is not themselves to a multitude of different depths – they clearly construct a world. However, the world that they construct is a boundaryless world; it is a world of pure feeling. This is not a world of distinct objects/parts.

The world of pure feeling is a world of different intensities of feeling, of different levels of embeddedness of feeling, and of different qualities of feeling. The world of pure feeling is characterised by shining beacons, by interconnections, and by attractions and repulsions. The world of pure feeling that is inhabited by feelings and things is not a world of space and time. To talk of the existence of a shining beacon in a world of pure feeling is to talk of the existence of an overpowering feeling. To be clear, in the Universal Feeling Body, the unobserved Universe, these very same shining beacons, and all nodes of feeling and things, exist in space and time; yet, in the world of pure feeling inhabited by feelings and things, there is no space and time – for, it is a world of pure feeling.

It is very important to appreciate that feelings and things do not have awareness of the world of pure feeling that they inhabit. Furthermore, it is also important to appreciate that whilst all feelings and things feel their own world, this world is far removed from the observed Universe of boundaries/objects/parts that is conceptually moulded by a speck.

The world of pure feeling is a feeling of the Universal Feeling Body.
And, just as every speck of thought/awareness has a unique
Universal Feeling Body, every feeling, and every thing, has a unique
world of pure feeling.

 # The sliding scale of embeddedness of a speck of thought/awareness

Let us explore the relationship between a speck of thought/awareness and its unique Universal Feeling Body. A speck of thought/awareness is differentially embedded with its Universal Feeling Body. That is to say, it is more embedded with some bits of its Universal Feeling Body, than it is with other bits of its Universal Feeling Body. More than this, it is not embedded with most of its Universal Feeling Body. Furthermore, there exists an enormous sliding scale of increasing and decreasing levels of embeddedness. A speck of thought/awareness is most deeply embedded with the animal body – for example, the head, torso, arms, and legs, of a human body – within which it intermittently emerges. It is also deeply embedded with the clothes that are worn by its animal body (if it wears clothes), the home of this body (if it has a home), and the places, the segments of the Universe, where it spends most of its time.

There is a need here to be clear. For, it is very important to appreciate
that there is a distinction between those segments of the Universe that
a speck of thought/awareness is embedded with, and those segments
of the Universe that constitute the Universal Feeling Body of a speck
of thought/awareness.

This distinction arises due to another distinction – nodes of feeling and things. At a given moment in time, a speck of thought/awareness will be embedded with a particular group of nodes of feeling; and, these nodes of feeling are themselves participants in an immense plethora of things. This means that when feeling gets radiated to embedded nodes from nodes of feeling that the speck is not embedded with, that the speck could become aware of this radiated feeling. So, if one envisions all of the nodes of feeling that a speck is embedded with, then all of the things that these nodes of feeling participate in will be encompassed within that speck of thought/awareness's Universal Feeling Body. For, all of the locations that originate feelings that a speck of thought/awareness can become aware of, are components of that speck of thought/awareness's Universal Feeling Body.

As a speck of thought/awareness moves through the Universal Feeling Body, the segments of the Universe – the nodes of feeling – that it is embedded with, inevitably changes. For, to put it extremely crudely and simplistically, such movement can cause low embeddedness to fall to zero embeddedness, zero embeddedness to become low embeddedness, medium embeddedness to become high embeddedness, and so on. Envision a speck of thought/awareness as a torch that is flowing through the Universe. At any point on its journey, that which is illuminated are the segments of the Universe, the nodes of feeling, that it is embedded with. And of that which is illuminated, some feelings will be much more illuminated than others; for, some of these feelings will be much more embedded with the speck of thought/awareness than others.

This torch analogy is useful, but not perfect. For, when the light from an actual torch moves, as the torch is carried along a path, that which is no longer illuminated in the present moment is in darkness. When an actual torch shines, the Universe surrounding the torch is either illuminated or not illuminated. When we envision a speck of thought/awareness as a torch, as an entity which emits a ray of light that illuminates, brings into awareness, particular bits of the Universal Feeling Body, what we are envisioning is that the current location of a speck is the ray of light, is those nodes of feeling that are very deeply embedded with the speck. This location will, of course, include its animal body, and it will also include the nodes of feeling that surround the animal body. When a speck of thought/awareness has a new location within the Universal Feeling Body – either through it moving, or due to the movements of that which is not itself – then a new bit of the Universal Feeling Body will be illuminated by the torch/speck, a bit that will still include the its unique travelling companion. Yet, unlike an actual torch, some nodes of feeling that were previously illuminated will still be embedded with the speck. For, that which was previously very deeply embedded, in the full glare of the rays of awareness/light, gradually becomes less embedded. These feeling nodes get increasingly less embedded, until their embeddedness with the speck falls to zero. Whilst these nodes are fading towards zero embeddedness they are still illuminated, but their luminosity is fading.

To get a handle on this, it might be very helpful to envision a speck of thought/awareness that is slowly moving around the entire coastline of a circular island. When it sets off on its journey from Point A it is deeply embedded with Point A. As it moves further and further away from Point A, it becomes increasingly less embedded with Point A, until it becomes unembedded with Point A. However, as the journey nears its completion, the speck starts to become embedded with Point A again. As the journey is completed, and the speck returns to its starting point, then it is, again, deeply embedded with Point A. A moving speck of thought/awareness, illuminating segments of the Universe as it flows through the Universal Feeling Body, like a torch illuminating the darkness of the night.

Let us remind ourselves that the embeddedness between a speck of thought/awareness and the Universal Feeling Body is a very different kind of phenomena to the embeddedness between nodes of feeling. The latter involves the forging and unforging of things, and is the domain of an animal body. The former type of embeddedness has a much narrower scope in terms of the segments of the Universe that are encompassed, and despite including bonds of very deep embeddedness, most of the connections that are formed tend to be more ephemeral. The latter type of embeddedness has a much broader scope, and whilst it encompasses a very wide variety of degrees of embeddedness between feelings, the connections that are formed are typically comparatively less ephemeral.

Let us explore this a little further. There are things – bonds of connection between feelings – which encompass the Moon and human bodies on the Earth. However, an Earth-based speck of thought/awareness is not embedded with the nodes of feeling that I conceptually mould into the Moon. This example throws light on the vast difference in scope between the two types of embeddedness.

The difference that exists in terms of ephemerality is largely grounded in the fact that specks of thought/awareness have a very short lifespan, whereas things can exist for thousands of years, millions of years, and much longer! This means that the embeddedness between nodes of feeling in things can be extraordinarily deep, when it is contrasted to the embeddedness between a speck of thought/awareness and nodes of feeling. This chasm in timespans also partially explains the vast difference in scope that pertains in the two different types of embeddedness; the other intertwining factor being that a speck of thought/awareness is tiny, whereas things can be tiny, medium-sized, or ginormous.

A brighter flowing torch within a dimmer flowing torch

Does what has just been discussed make sense to you? The nodes of feeling that constitute an animal body have been participating in things for millions of years. This means that animal bodies are embedded in an intricate manner with large swathes of the Earth and our Solar System; whereas, a speck will be very lucky if it exists for two hundred years. So, this means that a speck will be embedded with vastly less feeling nodes, and will be vastly less embedded with these nodes, than its animal body.

A speck of thought/awareness is exceptionally deeply embedded with its animal body. This means that a speck is highly sensitive to the feelings that exist in the segment of the Universe that it conceptually moulds as its animal body. In turn, this means that when feelings originate in nodes of feeling in any of the things that an animal body participates in, and consequently instantly radiate throughout these things, that the speck of thought/awareness that is located in the animal body can, possibly, become aware of these feelings when they radiate into the animal body. However, due to co-radiation throughout a thing, the high-level feelings which originate in the things that an animal body participates in will dominate these things. So, in these things, only the high-level feelings that originate outside of the animal body, along with the high-level feelings that originate inside the animal body, can possibly enter the awareness of the speck that is located in the animal body.

When we switch our attention to the embeddedness that exists between a speck and nodes of feeling that are located outside of its animal body, we can appreciate that the speck can become directly aware of some of the feelings that radiate to its animal body at their point of origination. However, a speck of thought/awareness cannot become directly aware of the vast majority of the feelings that radiate to its animal body at their point of origination; for, it isn't embedded with these nodes. In this case, the direct awareness of feeling nodes that are located outside of its animal body, it is possible for a speck of thought/awareness to become aware of non-high-level feelings.

When one envisions a speck of thought/awareness as a torch that flows through the Universe, then one can picture the segments that are currently illuminated to any degree as the nodes of feeling which the speck is currently embedded with to any degree, and therefore can potentially become directly aware of. In the realm of these embedded nodes, a speck of thought/awareness will typically become aware of either the feelings that it is currently the most deeply embedded with, or the feelings that are the most intense. Those feelings that are currently illuminated by the flowing torch are those feelings that the speck can possibly become aware of at their point of origination. Yet, this flowing torch is a flowing torch within a flowing torch. For, there is a much larger flowing torch, which is the speck's Universal Feeling Body. The Universal Feeling Body of a speck of thought/awareness can be thought of as a flowing torch which is comparatively very dim, and which encapsulates, houses inside itself, the much brighter flowing torch, which illuminates the nodes of feeling within its Universal Feeling Body that a speck can currently become directly aware of. That which is illuminated by the dimmer torch, but not the brighter torch, can only enter the awareness of a speck of thought/awareness by instantly radiating throughout things into that portion of the speck of thought/awareness's Universal Feeling Body that is currently illuminated by the brighter torch. And, that which radiates from the dimmer torch to the animal body of the speck is most likely to enter its awareness.

Are there things as large as our Solar System?

We have explored how there are tiny things and massive things. You know that things are networks of interconnected nodes of feeling that are equally embedded and which instantly co-radiate feelings throughout themselves. Our focus here is to start to address the issue of exactly how massive these things can be. Our question is: Are there things which encompass our entire Solar System?

It is obvious that the feelings of the Earth are heavily influenced by the feelings of the Sun. For, the feelings of the Sun reach the Earth in the form that we call 'sunlight'. Sunlight also permeates our entire Solar System. Yet, whilst such permeation points towards our Solar System as a singular entity, it does not entail the existence of things that encompass our entire Solar System. For, sunlight is the movement of feeling within the Universal Feeling Body, rather than the instant radiation of feeling throughout things.

We earlier explored *the feeling state of the Solar-Systic whole* which comes into being due to the massive shining beacons of feeling that humans conceptually mould as 'planets' coming into and out of particular arrangements. Our question is: Does *the feeling state of the Solar-Systic whole* entail the existence of things that encompass our entire Solar System? Our answer is: There are things that encompass our entire Solar System; and, the feeling state of these things gives rise to *the feeling state of the Solar-Systic whole*.

One can envision our Solar System as a feeling Sun which continuously radiates feelings to its collections of circling feelings (planets), and one can picture these collections of feelings perennially circling the Sun, getting closer to each other, moving away from each other; forever circling; forever continuously radiating feelings both to each other and to the Sun. From this perspective, one can picture our Solar System not as one thing, but as an extraordinarily ginormous number of things, things whose combined current qualitative feeling state is the current *feeling state of the Solar-Systic whole*. Another way of expressing what is going on here is to appreciate that each of the planets has a unique qualitative character, and that the arrangement of these planets vis-à-vis each other activates a unique feeling state of the whole – a state that is instantiated in the things that encompass the Solar System.

Is the Universe one thing? In other words, is the Universe the dimmer torch?

We can now explore whether the entire Universe is one thing. If the entire Universe is one thing, then it would be the case that the entire Universe is one's Universal Feeling Body. That is to say, rather than one's Universal Feeling Body being the dimmer torch that is flowing through the Universe, one's Universal Feeling Body would be the entire Universe.

One can envision the entire Universe as one feeling thing. However, we are here envisioning a thing whose embeddedness is so shallow, whose feeling intensity is so low, that it barely resembles the things that exist in animal bodies, the things that exist on the Earth, and the things that exist in our Solar System.

As the Universe continues to expand, the thing that is the Universe continues on its journey towards lessening embeddedness and lessening feeling. This is a journey without an end; for, the embeddedness will never fade to zero. That which feels cannot stop feeling, it can only feel progressively less. As the feeling in the thing that is the Universe fades, the *Stages of Universal Unfoldment* ensure that feeling intensity in the Universe continues to increase via the bringing forth of the movement patterns of small deeply embedded things, which includes the bringing into being of specks to steer animal bodies.

The storage of visual perceptions, auditory sensings, and auditory outputs

We have explored how feeling memories are stored within the Universal Feeling Body. When a feeling feels a feeling this encounter becomes etched into their nodes; that is to say, the nodes of feeling have a feeling memory of the feeling. Let us now explore how the mouldings of the visual sense, auditory sensings, and the outputs of the auditory sense, can also become stored as feeling memories in the nodes of feeling in the Universal Feeling Body that they are highly associated with. The mouldings of the visual sense are collections of parts. Auditory sensings are the feelings that are auditorily sensed. Auditory outputs are the interpretations of the feelings that are auditorily sensed, a subset of which is the interpretation of feelings as linguistic utterances.

Let's elucidate on what has just been said. The unobserved Universe is comprised of nodes of feeling. Feelings have the quality of feelings that they have due to feeling other feelings. The feeling of a feeling becomes etched into a feeling and in this way feeling memories exist in nodes of feeling. When an animal body auditorily senses feeling, this feeling becomes stored in the nodes of feeling that are deeply embedded with the auditory sensing. Furthermore, the auditory outputs that are created out of these sensings, which could be a string of words such as – *'Shall we go to Dartington Hall or The Old Postern'* – can also become stored in the nodes of feeling that are deeply embedded with the speck. Similarly, the visually perceived parts which have been conceptually moulded can become stored in the nodes that are deeply embedded with the speck of thought/awareness. These stored visual perceptions, auditory sensings, and auditory outputs, are an aspect of a feeling memory.

A rather gruesome example should amply illustrate this. Imagine that one is in a museum where one is drawn to a jumper that is on display. One's human body touches the jumper and one is instantly overcome with a feeling of intense pain, despair, and impending doom. More than this, one becomes aware of the sound of a 'blood-curdling scream', of the words 'you are going to die', and also has a vision of a knife coming towards one. This experience is likely to be rather unpleasant. Why did it occur? One was accessing the visual perceptions, auditory sensings, and auditory outputs of the speck/human that used to own the jumper. One will not be surprised when one discovers that the jumper was being worn by the victim of a mass murderer at the moment of their death.

It wasn't just the victim's feelings that got stored in the Universal Feeling Body; the accompanying auditory sensings, auditory outputs, and visual perceptions, also got stored. There is a reason why these particular perceptions/sensings/outputs came into one's awareness when one's human body touched the jumper: the feelings in which they are stored (or the feelings that they are, in the case of the auditory sensing) – the feelings that came into existence at the same time that the visual and auditory events occurred – are of such an exceptionally high intensity. Indeed, these will be the most intense feeling memories in the jumper.

A less gruesome scenario involves touching a musical instrument that was regularly used by a famous musician. When one's human body touches the instrument it wouldn't be a surprise if one had the vision of being on stage and peering out at a crowd of adoring fans. One might also become aware of song lyrics, the sound of 'clapping', and become aware of the feeling of immense exhilaration that the musician felt whilst performing. The touching of the instrument is very potent because it involves two phenomena. Firstly, a very high level of association between a speck and the feeling memories that are the instrument. Secondly, a very high level of association between the feelings of one's animal body and the feeling memories that are the instrument. It wouldn't be a surprise if one progressively experienced the phenomena outlined above more intensely as one got increasingly close to the instrument.

Animal actions – thoughts versus feelings

A speck of thought/awareness intermittently emerges in an animal body. In the following sections we have a very interesting issue to address. This issue is the nature of the relationship between a speck and the nodes of feeling in the Universal Feeling Body, when it comes to the causal factors which result in movements of the animal body, thoughts to come into existence, and feelings to come into existence. Do thoughts determine feelings? Do feelings determine thoughts? Or, do thoughts determine feelings and feelings determine thoughts? And, how do thoughts and feelings causally relate to the movements/actions of an animal body?

Feelings determine thoughts

You know from your own experience that the feelings that you become aware of determine your thoughts. When you become aware of feelings such as a rancid stench, a toothache, a horrible din, elation, a stinging sensation, extreme pain, bitterness, a cluster headache, sweetness, or pins and needles, you are naturally and inevitably drawn to think about these feelings. Feelings determine thoughts.

The causes of thought

Thoughts are not just determined by feelings. A thought can give rise to a thought. So, a thought can be caused by a thought or by a feeling. A thought can also arise due to a visual perception, or due to auditory outputs. A thought can also be not caused; it can just pop into existence without any causal antecedents, wholly self-generated as a stand-alone entity within a speck. So, a particular thought exists due to a feeling, another thought, a visual perception, the interpretation of the feelings that have been sensed by one's ears, or self-generation.

Thoughts do not determine feelings

Do thoughts determine feelings? Thoughts do not determine feelings. When a speck of thought/awareness has a thought this does not change states of feeling within the Universal Feeling Body. However, there is, of course, an indirect causal link from thoughts to feelings. For, a speck of thought/awareness can make decisions, and decisions often lead to an animal body moving/acting in a particular way. And, if an animal body moves, if it changes its location within the Universal Feeling Body, then its feelings will change. Any movement within the Universal Feeling Body causes a new set of feeling relationships to come into existence, as a cascade of new relationships of both increasing feeling association and reducing feeling association are forged.

In contrast, a speck of thought/awareness might decide *not* to move its animal body, and this decision will also lead to changes in feeling in its animal body. For, a non-moving animal body will be affected by the movements that surround that body. For instance, if the body of another animal moves closer to the speck of thought/awareness's animal body, and if the speck decides not to move its animal body in response to the approaching animal body, then the feelings in its own animal body will be changed. For, the approaching animal body is becoming an increasingly significant and potent component of the things in which the speck's animal body participates. These things, let us remind ourselves, are networks of feelings that permeate the Universal Feeling Body; networks which have little respect for the superficial boundaries that are moulded in an observed Universe – boundaries such as animal bodies.

We can quite easily appreciate that both the decision of a speck to move its animal body, and the decision not to do so, will result in the feelings in its animal body changing. For, any movements in the animal body itself, or in the things in which the animal body participates, will change the feelings in the animal body. Furthermore, it should be noted that there are processes of computation in animal brains which regulate and determine movements within the animal body. When a movement within an animal body is automatically initiated by computation, then this movement changes the feelings in the animal body. If a speck exists in the animal body, then it might become aware of this change in feeling; however, it plainly isn't the cause of the change.

The causes of actions/movements

The actions/movements of an animal body are typically, but not always, determined by thoughts. For, an action/movement can also be directly caused by a feeling, by a visual perception, or due to auditory outputs. Furthermore, and in accordance with this, animal bodies can sometimes operate in 'autopilot' mode, within which bodily movements are caused by *an established pattern of previous actions/movements* (habits). This means that current bodily movements are being caused by a previous pattern of thoughts / feelings / visual perceptions / auditory outputs; an established habitual way of acting/moving in a particular situation.

Movements/actions determine feelings – the Moon and the lunatic

Let us consider an animal body. Movements/actions determine feelings. Feelings determine thoughts. Thoughts determine movements/actions. This is a set of rather circular looking relationships.

All movements/actions determine feelings, from the bending of one's little finger, to the orbit of the Moon. In this respect, it is worth reflecting on the fact that the movements of the Moon change the states of feeling on the Earth, and this includes the feelings of the nodes of feeling that are animal bodies. In turn, this change in feeling affects the thoughts that specks of thought/awareness are having, which consequently determines the movements/actions of both human bodies and the bodies of non-human animals.

You will surely be aware that at Full Moon lots of humans act noticeably differently. Indeed, the word 'lunatic' was created to refer to widespread changes in human behaviour that regularly occurred at this stage of the lunar cycle. Now you have a greater understanding of why this is so.

Feeling is the fundamental force: Why does any entity move?

Feeling is the fundamental force which *causes* events to occur in the Universe. Feelings explain why the segments of the Universe interact in the way that they do – the movements of planets, physical interactions, chemical interactions, and the vast majority of biological interactions. Feeling doesn't explain all biological interactions because in biological entities that contain a speck of thought/awareness – Mode 3 segments of the Universe – there is an additional factor that needs to be taken into account: *Is this segment of the Universe acting/moving the way that it is due to its feeling interactions, or is it acting/moving the way that it is due to its speck of thought/awareness?* As we have explored, whilst a speck can initiate actions/movements, it is itself heavily influenced by feeling.

We can appreciate that the overwhelming majority of the Universal Feeling Body moves automatically in accordance with the feelings that exist at a particular moment in time. Animal bodies sometimes move in this automatic fashion. However, the movements of animal bodies can, in addition, be initiated by specks of thought/awareness. Through their indirect movements, specks of thought/awareness can also initiate movements in segments of the Universe that are located outside of their animal bodies. A speck of thought/awareness can initiate movements that are grounded in feelings, and it can also initiate movements that are wholly grounded in itself.

The causes of one's thoughts

As an 'I', as a speck of thought/awareness that is enmeshed within the Universal Feeling Body, one's thoughts are overwhelmingly determined by the following: the nodes of feeling in the Universal Feeling Body that one is deeply embedded with, one's previous thoughts, one's visual perceptions, and one's auditory outputs. However, one's thoughts will, to a much lesser extent, also be determined by the nodes of feeling in one's Universal Feeling Body that one is less embedded with. So, one's thoughts will be determined by factors such as the position of the Moon, because the feeling networks of the Moon extend to the Earth; that is to say, there are things that incorporate your human body and the Moon.

We also need to remind ourselves that the nodes of feeling within the Universal Feeling Body that have been deeply embedded with a speck of thought/awareness will contain feeling memories of visual perceptions, auditory sensings, and auditory outputs. What this means is that a speck can become aware of these feeling memories when it becomes deeply embedded with the nodes of feeling within which they are stored. In turn, this means that one's thoughts can be, to some degree, determined by the feeling memories which emanate from animal bodies and specks of thought/awareness that existed in the past. And, in a similar vein, if one is deeply embedded with other currently existing animal bodies and specks of thought/awareness, then awareness of their current visual perceptions, auditory sensings, auditory outputs, thoughts, and feelings, can also be a factor in determining one's thoughts.

You might recall that we previously explored how thoughts can become stored in nodes of feeling. It follows that if a speck of thought/awareness is deeply embedded with such feeling nodes, then these stored thoughts can, to some degree, determine its thoughts. Such thoughts can suddenly emerge and implant themselves within a process of thought/awareness. Of course, given what has already been said, one's feelings, and thus one's thoughts, will also be affected by *the feeling state of the Solar-Systic whole,* which we explored earlier.

Feelings are 'king'

What one feels one becomes. What one feels one thinks. What one thinks one becomes. When one's human body moves, the feelings in that body change. When the things in the Universal Feeling Body that one's human body participates in move, then the feelings in one's human body change. One's human body is in a constant state of becoming. Oneself – a speck of thought/awareness – is also in a constant state of becoming. The actions/movements of one's human body are primarily determined by one's thoughts and by the things that one's human body participates in.

Thoughts can be self-generated, divorced from feelings, but feelings are ultimately 'king' – the superior partner of the two phenomena. A speck of thought/awareness has free will: it has the ability to make different decisions in a given situation. However, if it continuously makes decisions that result in actions, or non-actions, which cause feelings of repulsion to come into existence, feelings that are not conducive to the health and wellbeing of the animal body within which it intermittently emerges, then that animal body will become unwell, and face a life of sickness, unhappiness, and early death.

A speck of thought/awareness ultimately has to take heed of the feelings that are its guide. These feelings are unique to a particular animal body; for, every speck of thought/awareness shines a light on, illuminates, a unique and specific portion of the Universal Feeling Body. These unique feelings are that which enables a speck of thought/awareness to steer and guide its animal body so that it flourishes and fulfils its unique potential.

The existence and nature of 'free will'

Let us explore the concept of 'free will'. I have stated that to say that a speck of thought/awareness has free will is to say that it *has the ability to make different decisions in a given situation.* You might be happy to accept that the existence of such an ability is worthy of the label 'free will'. After all, such a power seems to be an ability that exceeds mere computation. There are two aspects to animal brains. Animal brains are computation devices, but in addition to such computation abilities, brains intermittently bring into existence specks of thought/awareness. One could very reasonably believe that computation devices lack the ability to make different decisions in a given situation; whereas, specks have this ability. In other words, when a speck of thought/awareness is present then free will exists; whereas, when it is not present, then the animal is either inactive or acting on autopilot in a deterministic fashion.

However, you might want to delve deeper. After all, what exactly does it mean to talk of a 'given situation'? How many factors should one include in such a description? You might want to resist the notion of 'free will' by formulating an in-depth description of a 'given situation' which seeks to detail the plethora of factors that cause a particular speck of thought/awareness to make a particular decision in this situation. This description will entail attempting to trace causal antecedents backwards in time in an attempt to prove that the decision that was made could not have been different. In this way, one might reach the conclusion that 'free will' doesn't exist in any meaningful sense. If one starts such a description, then one seems to be heading down a bottomless rabbit hole, into the depths of the unanswerable abyss.

The attempt to trace causal antecedents backwards in time in order to show that free will doesn't exist is misguided. Why is this attempt misguided? The components of an animal brain that bring into existence a speck of thought/awareness – the movement pattern that generates a speck of thought/awareness, has causal antecedents; however, the speck of thought/awareness that is generated by this movement pattern does not have causal antecedents. *For, the emergence of a speck is a new beginning; it is not determined by that which came before.* A speck of thought/awareness has the ability to make different decisions in a given situation. A speck of thought/awareness has the ability to self-generate its thoughts. So, a speck of thought/awareness has free will. *More than this, a speck of thought/awareness is free will.*

The human auditory sense and the feelings of the chalkboard

In the following sections we will delve a little deeper into the auditory sense. What does the auditory sense sense? The auditory sense of one's human body directly senses one's Universal Feeling Body. That is to say, sounds are feelings. Everything that one hears is a feeling, a feeling that is located somewhere in one's Universal Feeling Body. Every thing that one hears has a particular feeling quality. You know that this is the case. You simply need to recall the feelings=sounds that come into existence when fingernails scratch a chalkboard. These feelings are powerful. Most human specks of thought/awareness find these feelings to be painful and distressing. When one becomes aware of these painful feelings, one is becoming aware of feelings that are located in one's body – located in one's Universal Feeling Body.

Sounds as feelings are sharply divorced from the attempt of a speck of thought/awareness to make sense of these feelings by categorising them. In other words, auditory outputs have no feeling content.

Where are the feelings that are auditorily sensed located?

When fingernails scratch a chalkboard feelings come into existence at this location. These feelings can be auditorily sensed. Auditory sensing is a structured activity, which means that these feelings can be sensed in different ways, and to different depths of feeling. One might want to ponder the issue of where the feelings that are auditorily sensed are located: Are they located at the site of the fingernails/chalkboard? Or, are they located in that which senses the feelings?

These questions are actually misplaced. For, as we previously explored, feelings do not just exist at one location. Nodes of feeling are participants in things, and the nodes of feeling in a thing are continuously instantly co-radiating feeling throughout themselves, thereby producing a singular feeling state of the thing. When one auditorily senses the feelings that come into existence when the movement of the fingernails on the chalkboard occurs, then one is sensing the feelings in things. In other words, the feelings that one is auditorily sensing exist at the site of the fingernails/chalkboard, they exist in the ears of one's human body, and they exist throughout the rest of their things. As one's human body typically participates deeply in the things that it auditorily senses, this means that the things that are sensed are typically high-level feelings.

One's human body is truly embedded within, enmeshed in, networks of feelings. This is what it means to be a speck of thought/awareness that has a Universal Feeling Body.

"You are in trouble"

From your own experience you will be very familiar with the distinction between the linguistic content of uttered words, and the feeling content of uttered words. Think of a sequence of words that you have heard, or imagine a sequence that you might hear. Perhaps: "I want you", or "I love you", or "you are in trouble".

These same words can be spoken, can be audibly created as feelings, with very different feeling content. At the extremes, there can be a feeling content that is menacing/dark/creepy/scary/freaky/repulsive, or a feeling content that is loving/gentle/kind/attractive. The former feeling content is likely to be created by a deranged homicidal stalker when they utter the words "you are in trouble". Whereas the latter feeling content is likely to be created by a concerned parent when they utter the words "you are in trouble".

The meaning of uttered words is to be found in their feeling content

The feeling content of vocal creations, of that which comes out of the mouths of humans, and of other animals, is a portion of the Universal Feeling Body. These feelings speedily move through the Universal Feeling Body, and as they speedily move they also continuously instantly radiate throughout things. These moving and radiating feelings are detectable by the ears of animals. Following this detection, a speck creates auditory outputs, it categorises the feelings, and some of these auditory outputs will be strings of words. These auditory outputs that arise from vocal creations are divorced from the feeling content of the uttered words. The same sequence of uttered words can be imbued with very different feeling. When a speck of thought/awareness entertains a sequence of words, in the form of an auditory output, it is more concerned with their feeling content than with the words themselves. The feeling content contains the truth, the reality, the real meaning, of the words.

Uttered words without feeling content are an impossibility, but if they were possible they would be hopeless, of no use whatsoever to a speck of thought/awareness. If this is not blatantly obvious to you, you can re-read the previous section. You might want to try and find exceptions to this rule, to recall situations in which the feeling content of uttered words was not essential in order to appreciate the meaning of what is being communicated. If one sets off on this endeavour, then the more that one tries, the more that one will come to realise the futility of one's endeavour. The real meaning of uttered words is to be found in their feeling content.

Visual perceptions are conceptual mouldings of structured sensings

Let us turn to visual perception. In contrast to that which is auditorily sensed, that which is visually sensed is not the Universal Feeling Body; that is to say, that which is sensed is not feelings/things. That which is visually sensed is a medium-grained construction, a structured sensing, of the movements of the Universal Feeling Body. The sensed movements are conceptually moulded by a speck and are thereby turned into the observed Universe of parts that is visually perceived. Visual perceptions are conceptual mouldings of structured sensings of the movements of the Universal Feeling Body; they are mouldings of that which feels; they are creators of apparent divisions in that which is undivided. Particular colours are perceived on particular objects in particular places.

Apparent non-movement is due to the structure of a visual sensing

You know that the visual sense does not directly sense feelings; it senses the movements of feelings. All of the feelings in the Universal Feeling Body are continuously moving, yet to a speck there can appear to be non-movement. The apparent non-movement of that which is moving is possible because of the structured nature of visual sensing.

Envision a particular segment of the Universe. Perhaps one can imagine that segment that the speck in a human might conceptually mould as 'a tree'. This segment can simultaneously be visually sensed as both moving and non-moving. Let us assume that when a human body visually senses this segment of the Universe that it detects an array of movement patterns. Yet, a coarser medium-grained visual sensing, by a non-human animal, can, at the same moment in time, detect non-movement in this same segment. This stark discrepancy between detected movement and detected non-movement provides very different foundations for the two specks of thought/awareness in the two animal bodies to conceptually mould what has been visually sensed. The speck in the human body will conceptually mould parts such as 'trunk gently swaying', 'leaves vigorously rustling', and 'branches slowly bending'. Whereas, the speck in the non-human animal body will conceptually mould a single part that encompasses this segment.

If you reflect on all of this, you will surely conclude that it is obvious. Yet, whilst it is obvious, the implications are immense – the observed Universe of an animal is created by that animal in a profound way. In the unobserved Universe there are no 'trees', there are just feeling movements. These movements can be visually sensed by different animal bodies in an immense plethora of ways. This means that what is in a continuous state of movement can appear to be not moving. This also means that a particular segment of the Universe can simultaneously appear, to different specks, to be both moving and non-moving. This is possible due to the unique way that the specks of thought/awareness forge their observed Universes of parts out of that which has been differentially visually sensed.

The animal body is bathed in light waves

There is more going on in visual sensing than meets the eye.

When an animal body is visually sensing the movements of the Universal Feeling Body its entire animal body is being bathed, drenched, saturated, in light waves. And light waves are, of course, waves of feeling. So, when the feelings that are light waves hit a human body, they are hitting toes, fingers, legs, arms, chest, and head, and they are interacting with the feelings that are these bits of the human body. A multitude of new feelings are forged.

A tiny fraction of the light waves that hit an animal body hit its eyes. This means that when visual sensing is occurring, waves of feeling are continuously streaming into an animal's eyes. Feeling interactions are occurring in the eyes; new feelings are forged. Typically these feelings are rather bland. However, on rare occasions these feelings can be high intensity feelings that are characterised by extreme discomfort. Indeed, terms have been coined to refer to this phenomenon: 'discomfort glare' and 'light sensitivity'.

Partial glimpses

The feelings of these four senses – the auditory sense, the sense of smell, the sense of taste, and the sense of touch – are the fundamental nature of the Universe. In other words, they are the Universal Feeling Body – the unobserved Universe. These senses, as distinct boundaried entities, only exist in an observed Universe, and they are limited access points, providers of partial glimpses, into the feelings that constitute a speck of thought/awareness's Universal Feeling Body. If a speck can become aware of a feeling, then that feeling is in its Universal Feeling Body.

To say that the unobserved Universe is unobservable is to say that it cannot be visually observed; for, the visual sense does not provide an access route to the Universal Feeling Body itself. It should be clearly understood that the unobserved Universe cannot be taken in, beholden, as a whole entity, by any sense of any animal body. The Universal Feeling

Body, once encountered through partial glimpses, can be increasingly known by a speck, but as a whole entity it can only be envisioned.

The ostracization of the human body from the Universal Feeling Body

In contrast to the other four senses, that which is visually perceived is superficial. The parts that are visually perceived are all conceptual mouldings that originate from a speck, and which collectively generate a particular appearance, a particular observed Universe. Yet, on the Earth, contemporary human culture, contemporary human life, is dominated by the visual sense. Such domination partially explains the phenomenon that is the widespread contemporary ostracization of the human body from the Universal Feeling Body – the sense of otherness, separation, and alienation, which marks the contemporary human condition.

The two routes to the existence of feelings within an animal body, and reaching outside of the animal body

A little more can be said in order to further clarify the nature of the relationship between a speck and its Universal Feeling Body. A speck of thought/awareness intermittently emerges in an animal body, and this animal body is the segment of the Universe which the speck is the most deeply embedded with. This is due to the extent of the two factors which increase association/embeddedness – closer spatial proximity and increasing temporal duration at a closer spatial proximity. Due to the immense depth of its embeddedness with its animal body, most of the feelings that a speck becomes aware of will be located in its animal body.

The last sentence requires immediate clarification. For, the animal body participates in a plethora of things which transcend the boundaries of the animal body. These things constitute the speck of thought/awareness's Universal Feeling Body. This means that there are two different routes to the existence of feelings within an animal body. Firstly, feelings come into existence within the animal body itself, from where they radiate throughout their things. Secondly, feelings originate outside of the animal body and get radiated into the animal body via the co-radiation of feelings throughout a thing.

In addition, a speck of thought/awareness can reach outside of the conceptually moulded part in its observed Universe that is its animal body, and thereby become directly aware of feelings which exist in certain bits of its broader Universal Feeling Body. This isn't surprising; for, the most fundamental body of a speck of thought/awareness is its Universal Feeling Body. The animal body is merely a superficial creation.

 # The subset of feelings in a speck of thought/awareness's Universal Feeling Body

Every animal body participates in an immense plethora of things – a ginormous number of networks – each of which is equally-embedded within itself. The totality of these things constitutes the Universal Feeling Body of the speck that intermittently emerges in an animal body.

The speck that emerges in an animal body will, at any moment in time, only be embedded with a small subset of the feelings that constitute its Universal Feeling Body. This subset is that collection of nodes of feeling which it can become directly aware of. It is important to appreciate that a speck of thought/awareness will be differentially embedded with the feelings in this subset. We have previously explored this distinction by envisioning the segments of the Universe that are illuminated by two torches. A speck of thought/awareness's Universal Feeling Body can be envisioned as the nodes of feeling that are illuminated by a dimmer torch; and, this torch contains within its area of illumination a smaller area that is differentially illuminated by a brighter torch. This smaller area equates to the nodes of feeling in the subset.

Body A, Speck A, Body B, Feeling B

It will be useful to put some flesh on the bones/nodes by considering a scenario that involves dual deep embeddedness. This is an instance of deep embeddedness both in terms of the level of the embeddedness of the nodes of feeling in things, and in terms of the level of embeddedness between a speck of thought/awareness and the nodes of feeling in the subset of its Universal Feeling Body that it can become directly aware of.

Let us envision a particular human body. We can call this human body: Body A. We can call the speck of thought/awareness that intermittently exists in this body: Speck A. We can use the phrase Body B to refer to a segment of the Universe that Body A and Speck A are deeply embedded with (Body B could, for example, be the spouse of Body A). This deep embeddedness means that the nodes of feeling in Body A and Body B participate in a multitude of deeply embedded things. We can call a feeling state that originates in a node of feeling in Body B: Feeling B. Feeling B will be in Speck A's subset.

When Feeling B originates in Body B, as the nodes of feeling in Body B are deeply embedded with Speck A – are in its subset – Speck A can become immediately aware of the existence of Feeling B in Body B. This awareness will most typically occur when Feeling B is very intense. In this scenario, Speck A is becoming aware of a state of feeling – Feeling B – that *originated* outside of Body A and which *exists* outside of Body A. *To appreciate what is going on here, it is perhaps useful to recall that every node of feeling has a unique feeling state due to it participating in a unique collection of things, whilst each thing has a singular feeling state due to the instant co-radiation of feeling throughout a thing.*

Now, something else is going on in tandem to this. As Body A is deeply embedded with Body B, the nodes of feeling in Body A and Body B jointly participate in a plethora of deeply embedded things. When Feeling B originates in Body B it instantly radiates throughout these things thereby modifying the feelings throughout these things. This means that the feeling impact of Feeling B is felt in Body A. Due to this transmission of the feeling, Speck A can become aware of the existence of Feeling B in Body A. So, Speck A is, in this case, becoming aware of a feeling that *exists* in its human body – Body A – but which *originated* outside of Body A. Yet, the feeling that exists in Body A is not Feeling B; rather, it is the feeling that has come into existence as Feeling B participated in the process of co-radiation throughout its things, thereby producing the singular feeling state of each of these things.

The process of co-radiation means that if Feeling B is the most intense feeling in a thing, that it will dominate this thing. Such domination means that it would largely shape the feeling of the thing. In an extreme case of domination, it would be hard to distinguish Feeling B in Body B from 'Feeling B' in Body A. Whereas, if Feeling B were to be the least intense feeling in a thing, then it would be dwarfed in the process of co-radiation, and the existence of Feeling B would be hard to detect in this thing in Body A. Yet, Feeling B would still be playing some role, however small, in shaping the feeling of this thing.

To put all of this more straightforwardly, Speck A can become aware of Feeling B in Body B, and it can also become aware of a feeling that to some degree approximates Feeling B in Body A. Furthermore, the degree of this approximation is dependent upon the extent to which Feeling B either dominates, or is dwarfed by, the other nodes of feeling in the things.

Simultaneous simplicity and complexity

The nature of the Universal Feeling Body is both immensely simple, and staggeringly intricate and complex, when it comes to the relationships between its nodes of feeling.

Rapidly changing torrents of feeling

At times you, as a speck of thought/awareness with a Universal Feeling Body, will find yourself in a relatively calm/stable flow of feeling. At other times, you will find yourself engulfed in a torrent of rapidly changing feeling. Being engulfed in such a torrent can be either invigorating or distressing. However, such engulfment is more likely to be invigorating.

Imagine your human body being battered by a hurricane, being pelted by rain, being under a powerful shower, cruising along a motorway on a motorbike or in a car, being on the beach as a tsunami makes landfall, being at a rock concert, or being on the crater of a volcano as it erupts – rumbling, hissing, exploding, roaring, immense heat, radiating gases, and surging pyroclastic flows. In all of these situations you are at the centre of a rapidly changing torrent of feeling. You are engulfed by this ever-changing stream, and your human body is typically enlivened and stimulated by its flow. Like a baby in the womb of its mother, both engulfed and enlivened by its interactions with its mother. A speck of thought/awareness engulfed not by the womb of its mother, but by the powerful streams of feeling of its Universal Feeling Body.

As your human body steps out from under the shower, as the hurricane passes, as the rock concert ends, as the volcano stops erupting, the enlivening/invigorating rapidly changing torrent of feeling is replaced with a calmer, slower, less frenetic flow of feeling.

When your human body is being pelted by rain, or drenched in sunlight, or permeated by loud music, you know that the feelings that you become aware of are heightened. However, you might have rationalised, or more likely just unquestioningly assumed, that the feelings in your human body were being heightened and invigorated by phenomena that were non-feeling. You might unquestioningly assume that: 'the rain is not itself feeling', 'the sunlight is not itself feeling', and 'the music is not itself feeling'. Why are you likely to unquestioningly assume this?

This 'non-feeling' assumption naturally arises out of the contemporary ostracization of the human body from the Universal Feeling Body, which we have already encountered.

It could be a radical change for you to come to appreciate that the feelings in your human body are being changed by feelings – rain is feeling, sunlight is feeling, music is feeling. Being drenched in sunlight entails the feelings that are sunlight interacting with the feelings that are a human body. The interaction of the two sets of feelings creates new states of feeling in the sunlight / human body, and these feelings instantly radiate throughout the things in which the sunlight / human body participates.

The human body is a beacon of feeling

The human body is a beacon of feeling. The human body is enmeshed in a web of feeling. Feeling is continuously pouring into one's human body, through one's human body, whilst also emanating from one's human body. That which is emanated is precious – it is high-level feeling, which includes the glorious zenith that is high intensity feeling.

Feeling is forging one's human body and transforming one's human body. Furthermore, the feeling that emanates from one's human body transforms its surroundings. When a human body walks, when it talks, when it breathes, when it moves, when it doesn't move, it is forging feeling connections. Feeling connections are forged and new feelings thereby radiate through the Universal Feeling Body in accordance with the degree of association between nodes of feeling. In other words, new feelings differentially instantly radiate throughout things – networks of equally-embedded feelings.

The Universal Feeling Body is not changed through the act of observation

The Universal Feeling Body is the unobserved Universe; it is what the Universe is like when it is not observed. The Universal Feeling Body still exists when the Universe is observed. Furthermore, the Universal Feeling Body cannot be observed, and it is also not changed through the act of observation. The transformation of the unobserved Universe into an observed Universe of parts does not change the unobserved Universe.

An observed Universe is a particular world of divisions and boundaries that a perceiver inevitably perceives. A visual sensing cannot sense the Universal Feeling Body; a perceiver cannot visually perceive the Universal Feeling Body. All that can possibly be sensed are the movements that emanate from the feeling interactions of the Universal Feeling Body. And the movement patterns that are sensed are dependent on the structure of the sensory apparatus.

The intricately interconnected web of differentially embedded feeling that sometimes contains specks of thought/awareness is not changed through the act of observation. For, to observe is simply to observe. Change in the Universe occurs due to movement and the passage of time. Observation exists in the realm of non-movement and occurs in the present moment. A speck is brought into being by a pattern of movement, but when it observes it does not move, does not change, that which it observes.

Quantum mechanics

Let us briefly ponder the relationship between quantum mechanics and the Universal Feeling Body. There are two reasons for doing this. Firstly, there are aspects of quantum mechanics that seem to shed light on, and tally with, aspects of the Universal Feeling Body. Secondly, multiple possible interpretations of quantum mechanics have been formulated, and it is possible that coming to know the Universal Feeling Body might shed light on which of these interpretations, if any, is true.

When one ponders one's observed Universe of parts, then one naturally thinks about classical physics, which studies matter and energy on the scale that is familiar to one's experience of one's observed Universe. When one switches to quantum mechanics – the study of matter and energy on the scale of atomic and subatomic particles – then one is still in the realm of the observed Universe of parts that is forged by humans. However, when one descends into the depths of an observed Universe in this way, then one is journeying towards the Universal Feeling Body. From these depths, one might even be able to glean some intellectual glimpses into certain aspects of the Universal Feeling Body.

Let us summarise some of the central features of the Universal Feeling Body. The Universal Feeling Body is an interconnected boundaryless web of feeling that is constituted out of feeling connections – bonds between feelings – some of which are extremely robust and some of which are very fragile. These connections constitute the things that are dispersed throughout the interconnected boundaryless web. Feeling connections establish feeling memories. Feelings feel each other, respond to each other, and recognise each other. A feeling arises in a node of feeling that has a particular location, a location which participates in a ginormous number of things, and it is instantly radiated throughout these networks. Feelings continuously radiate from their point of origin in accordance with their associations; that is to say, feelings continuously differentially instantly radiate throughout their things; deeply embedded nodes share more of their feeling than weakly embedded nodes. Every node of feeling in a thing is simultaneously radiating its feeling to every other node of feeling in a thing. This is the phenomenon of co-radiation throughout a thing which gives rise to a singular feeling within a thing. Yet, every node of feeling has unique feeling due to participating in a unique bundle of things. The Universal Feeling Body, as a boundaryless web of feeling, does not contain distinct objects. For an object to exist, the Universal Feeling Body has to be moulded into a part through visual perception. Yet, visual sensing and conceptual moulding does not change the Universal Feeling Body itself. Furthermore, if we envision a particular segment of the Universe, this bit of the Universal Feeling Body can be simultaneously moulded into a plethora of different parts/objects, by a plethora of diverse visual perceptions. Finally, the entire Universe is one extremely weakly associated minimally feeling thing.

Let us now consider the various interpretations of quantum mechanics. These interpretations have different takes on issues such as whether a sensing of the Universe collapses the wavefunction from a state of superposition into a definite singular state, whether reality is local or nonlocal, whether there are many worlds or just one world, and whether in addition to the wavefunction actual configurations of particles exist in the unobserved Universe. When one comes to know the Universal Feeling Body – the instant radiation of feeling throughout things, a boundaryless collection of networks that is unchanged by observation, yet which can simultaneously be moulded into a plethora of 'worlds' by diverse visual perceptions – then one can approach these various interpretations from a different perspective.

In this light, we are now ready to consider how visual perception, in the process of creating an observed Universe, eliminates the fuzziness of the unobserved Universe in a particular way, without changing the Universal Feeling Body. This exploration will enable us to appreciate how multiple observed Universes can simultaneously exist.

The elimination of fuzziness and the simultaneous existence of multiple observed Universes

We have explored how, in order for there to be a distinct object within the boundaryless web that is the Universal Feeling Body, there needs to be a boundary that is created by an act of conceptual moulding by a speck. A boundary, a delineated object, a part, such as a 'cat', or a 'tree', needs to be conceptually moulded in order to exist as an entity that is delineated from its surroundings. And a conceptual moulding follows a structured visual sensing. In the absence of conceptual moulding, all that exists in the Universe are nodes of feeling, and possibly also specks of thought/awareness. Nodes of feeling move in particular patterns, which can be visually sensed as a diversity of different movement patterns in accordance with the sensory structure of that which senses. The various movement patterns that exist in the unobserved Universe are different to the movement patterns that are structurally visually sensed. A particular movement pattern of nodes in the unobserved Universe brings into being a speck. So, if this pattern exists, then a speck exists.

As we have explored, the unobserved Universe, the Universal Feeling Body, does not change when it is observed, when it is visually sensed and conceptually moulded. Such sensing and moulding does not change the location of feelings, the quality of feelings, or the continuously radiating flows of feeling, and it does not affect the existence or non-existence of specks of thought/awareness within the Universal Feeling Body.

It is important to appreciate that visual sensing is a structured activity. That which can possibly be sensed is determined by the structure of the visual sense itself. The bringing of a particular structure is the imposition, the laying, of this particular structure onto that which is unstructured. In other words, the Universal Feeling Body is boundaryless; it is simply an interconnected matrix of flowing nodes of radiating feeling. Within this matrix there are various movement patterns, but such variety does not establish boundaries. The structure that is imposed on the Universal Feeling Body through a visual sensing does not itself mould the Universal Feeling Body into distinct objects/parts; it simply provides a framework within which a speck attempts to make sense of what is sensed. This process of making sense results in conceptual mouldings – the bringing forth of boundaries, concepts, distinct isolated objects, parts – within a speck. In this way, parts such as a 'cat', a 'microphone', a 'tree', and a 'table', are brought into being in an observed Universe.

So, visual perception is a two-stage activity – a structured visual sensing that is intertwined with a conceptual moulding. This two-stage activity underpins the simultaneous existence of multiple observed Universes. Due to visual perception being a two-stage activity, there are two ways in which unique observed Universes are brought into being.

Firstly, the structure of the visual sensory apparatus can be immensely different. In this respect, is it is very useful to contrast the visual sensory apparatus of humans, pigs, bees, mice, fish, alligators, beetles, eagles, dolphins, crows, pigeons, and seahorses. These diverse animals construct and inhabit very different observed Universes. We earlier explored these diverse visual sensory structures in these two sections: # *Is it a kangaroo, a flock of birds, or the Solar System? # Medium-grained sensing.*

Secondly, conceptual mouldings of similar visual sensings, even identical visual sensings, can be very different. In order to get a handle on this, it is useful to envision a collection of human bodies. Let us assume that all of these bodies have an identical visual sensory apparatus. We can then explore how each of these humans can inhabit a unique observed Universe of parts through having different conceptual mouldings. That is to say, each of the specks in this collection of human bodies conceptually carves up what is visually sensed differently. In order to appreciate how this occurs, it will be fruitful to compare both humans that live in very different cultures, and humans who live at different times in history.

Envision how the conceptual mouldings of a speck in a human body that inhabits New York might differ from the conceptual mouldings of the speck of an Eskimo who lives in the Arctic Circle. Furthermore, consider how these conceptual mouldings might radically differ from those of the speck in a human body that lives in an Amazonian tribe. The conceptual mouldings of these three specks can be very different.

A well known example of this is that Eskimos, uniquely, have an immense array of different conceptual mouldings of the segments of the Universe that most humans simply call 'snow'. What this means is that if our three specks were to be presented with identical visual sensings of a particular segment of the Universe, that the speck in the Eskimo could conceptually mould it into thirty different parts, whereas the specks in the New Yorker and the Amazonian could both conceptually mould just one part. The speck of thought/awareness in the Eskimo is clearly creating a very different observed Universe to the other two specks.

Perhaps a better way to try and appreciate what is going on here is to picture a human that was alive two thousand years ago. Let us imagine that this human lived their entire life in the segment of the Universe that we call 'London'. Try and envision the conceptual mouldings that the speck of thought/awareness in this human forged out of its visual sensings, the parts that existed in its observed Universe two thousand years ago. After one has done this, one can then imagine that this human was transported through time and emerged in the centre of London in the year 2024. The speck would be in a state of total disarray and confusion; it would be totally baffled and overwhelmed; its human body is visually sensing its surroundings, but it cannot possibly comprehend or make sense of these sensings.

What is being visually sensed might not be confusing to you, for you are surely familiar with the conceptual mouldings that are: cars, headphones, trains, mobile phones, traffic lights, airplanes, helicopters, skyscrapers, roads, the London Underground, motorbikes, trams, buses, credit cards, television screens, drones, earbuds, electric skateboards, cameras, and vapes. However, you can surely easily appreciate that in this situation the human that was transported from the 1st century AD would be in a state of disarray; for, their speck of thought/awareness lacks the conceptual framework to be able to make any sense of the visual sensings that it is presented with. Consequently, the conceptual mouldings of this speck, and thus the observed Universe of this human, would be immensely different from that of another human that is also in London in the year 2024, but who was born in London in the year 2000 AD.

You might recall that earlier in our explorations into the Universal Feeling Body we imagined encountering an alien planet which was initially a baffling undecipherable mess of intermingling stuff. Such an encounter is very analogous to the scenario that we have just considered. For, from the perspective of a human speck that existed two thousand years ago, the centre of London in 2024 would be a truly alien world.

So, visual perception is a two-stage activity which results in the bringing into being of a plethora of different observed Universes. That which is boundaryless is first given structure through a structured visual sensing, and is then conceptually moulded. When an observed Universe comes into being it is continuously in a definite single state for an observer. An act of visual perception brings into being a definite singular state – a particular observed Universe – without changing the state of the unobserved Universe itself. For, the definite singular state is generated by the observer; it is generated within the observer. So, this means that if there are simultaneous multiple acts of observation, arising in diverse animal bodies, then a multiplicity of very diverse observed Universes can concurrently exist. In other words, there is one Universal Feeling Body, and there are multiple observed Universes. That which is one, is perceived as many.

You might be finding it hard to envision what these words are attempting to convey. We are talking about bringing boundaries, definite edges, to that which lacks boundaries/edges. Perhaps it might help to think of the unobserved Universe as 'fuzzy', or as like a mass of candy floss; it is a collection of observer-independent movement patterns: the Universal Moving Body. A visual perception, in bringing definite edges, eliminates the fuzziness in a particular way, a way that is dependent on the nature of both the visual sensing and the conceptual moulding. Nodes of feeling, connections between feelings, things which are dispersed through space, feelings that are continuously co-radiating throughout things, constitute the interconnected flowing matrix that is the Universal Feeling Body. And it is this which underpins that which appears as a part in a particular place.

A fruitful way of envisioning the elimination of fuzziness, the creation of boundaries, is to attempt to envision the movements that are occurring in the unobserved Universe. Envision one undivided entity which has a plethora of diverse movements within itself. From the perspective of the observed Universe of divisions, one might refer to some of these movements as: 'rain falling', 'bird flying', 'scissors cutting', 'human walking', 'tiger running', 'helicopter flying', 'pen writing', 'fish swimming', 'planet circling', 'pendulum swinging', and 'water gushing'. From the perspective of the unobserved Universe, all of these movements are simply movements within one boundaryless entity. This is, in some ways, analogous to the beating of the heart, the breathing of the lungs, the digestion of food, and the circling of blood, within one animal body.

There is more to be said; for, the particular movement patterns that are visually sensed are sensed due to the structure of that which senses. The unobserved Universe is really one giant fuzzy movement pattern; and, the particular patterns that are visually sensed within this one giant fuzzy movement pattern are determined by the structure of a particular visual sense. A visual sense could sense the movement pattern that is 'human body running'. A different visual sense could be 'blind' to this movement pattern, whilst sensing the movement pattern that is 'food digesting', or 'heart beating', or 'lungs expanding and contracting', or 'blood circling'. And, a speck of thought/awareness can only conceptually mould that which has been visually sensed.

The fuzzy intermingling movements in the unobserved Universe can be carved up in an immense number of different ways, through different visual sensings and conceptual mouldings, as fuzziness gives way to a multitude of observed Universes that are in definite singular states. The elimination of fuzziness is the bringing into existence of an observed Universe which has a particular mosaic of parts; a mosaic of parts that is brought into being within a specific observer, due to the particular visual perceptions of that observer.

Specks of thought/awareness are not fuzzy

Specks of thought/awareness, like nodes of feeling, exist in the realm of the unobserved Universe; this means that their existence is not observer-dependent. Furthermore, the phenomenon of fuzziness does not apply to specks of thought/awareness. Indeed, specks of thought/awareness are the only bits of the Universal Feeling Body that are not fuzzy. Feelings are fuzzy. Things are fuzzy. The movements that are generated by the interactions of nodes of feeling are fuzzy. Whatever can be observed is fuzziness masquerading as non-fuzziness.

Colours are uninteresting

Colours are quite pleasant to behold, but they are uninteresting; for, they are aspects of the superficial observed Universe of parts. Whilst, our exploration is into the fundamental nature of the Universe: the Universal Feeling Body.

When a particular movement pattern of nodes is visually sensed by a particular movement pattern of nodes, then a particular colour is sensed. If one knows the movement patterns, then one knows the colour. This is very uninteresting.

There is perhaps one noteworthy thing to be said about colours. Green. The colour green. For, in my observed Universe, on the overwhelming majority of occasions that I visually perceive the colour green, I am indirectly visually perceiving medium-level feelings: that which is living without thought/awareness. This apparent correspondence between the colour green and medium-level feelings is seemingly an aspect of the existence of colours that is interesting. For, the movement patterns of medium-level feelings, when visually sensed by my human body, seem to correspond to the movement patterns of the colour green.

Distinctive movements within a continuously moving whole

Movements are much more interesting than colours! For, movements are intimately connected to feelings. Any movement in the Universal Feeling Body entails a change in feeling. Movements are either caused by feelings, or by that which does not feel: specks of thought/awareness.

Furthermore, whilst the Universal Feeling Body is a boundaryless whole, we can very fruitfully approach it from the perspective of the distinctive movements that are occurring in different locations within the whole. Movements which, from the scale and structure of visual sensing that is involved in human visual sensing, could be visually sensed and conceptually moulded as: 'candle burning', 'tiger running', 'helicopter blades rotating', 'raindrops falling', 'airplane flying', 'knife chopping', 'water flowing', 'human walking', 'tree leaves rustling', 'planet rotating', 'beaver burrowing', 'elephants stampeding', 'scissors cutting', 'high jump jumper jumping', 'shooting star shooting', 'kangaroo leaping', and 'Tyrannosaurus Rex running'. These conceptually moulded parts point at distinctive movements that are occurring in the Universal Feeling Body – the unobserved Universe – irrespective of whether or not they are boundaried and isolated via a visual sensing and a conceptual moulding.

Is this making sense to you? From the perspective of the Universal Feeling Body it makes perfect sense to talk about the existence of the distinctive movements that one might call 'tigers running', 'beavers burrowing', and 'helicopter blades rotating', even though there are no distinct objects, no parts, no boundaried entities, that answer to the name 'tiger', 'beaver', or 'helicopter'. These movements are simply distinctive movements within a continuously moving whole.

When a speck of thought/awareness beholds the movements of the Universal Feeling Body it seeks to impose order, it strives its best to make sense of that which is visually sensed, and it does this by isolating and conceptualising particular movement patterns. *That which moves like 'x' is 'raindrops falling'. That which moves like 'y' is 'tiger running'.* Such conceptualised movement patterns underpin the observed Universe of parts that is forged by a speck of thought/awareness. Parts arise from either movement patterns – how an entity is moving, or from a belief as to how an entity could possibly move.

It is very important to realise that movement patterns are related to the three levels of feeling and the *Stages of Universal Unfoldment.* For, there are distinctive movement patterns that distinguish collections of nodes of low-level feelings, from collections of nodes of medium-level feelings, from collections of nodes of high-level feelings. That is to say, when the inanimate brings into being that which is living without thought/awareness, then the Universe has evolved new distinctive movement patterns within the moving whole. And, when that which is living without thought/awareness brings into being that which is living with thought/awareness, then the Universe has evolved new and even more distinctive movement patterns within the moving whole.

Technological movements and the search for human-like aliens

The tight relationship between distinctive movement patterns, the three levels of feeling, and the *Stages of Universal Unfoldment,* becomes more complex when the *Stages of Universal Unfoldment* approach their zenith, within the final stage of unfoldment. For, the movement patterns of the technological creations of humans are collections of nodes of low-level feelings. Yet, movement patterns such as 'helicopter blades rotating' are movement patterns which clearly indicate that the *Stages of Universal Unfoldment* have reached the advanced stage of high-level feelings – the advanced stage of living with thought/awareness. For, only such advanced entities – exceptionally complex movement patterns of nodes of feeling which are steered and guided by specks of thought/awareness in which awareness participates in highly complex thought – can bring forth into existence the movement pattern that is 'helicopter blades rotating'. If such a movement pattern exists in any segment of the Universe, then it indicates that the *Stages of Universal Unfoldment* in this segment have reached the advanced stage of high-level feelings – the advanced stage of living with thought/awareness.

So, the search for human-like aliens in the rest of the Universe is the search for particular types of movement pattern. If the movement pattern that is 'helicopter blades rotating' is discovered in a distant galaxy, then this is a sure sign that human-like aliens exist there.

The intermediary – the giant borderless movement pattern

Movement patterns are an intermediary between the Universal Feeling Body and an observed Universe. Feelings have specific attractions and repulsions to other feelings and they consequently interact in particular ways; that is to say, their nodes move in particular ways. When there is a structured visual sensing, these movements are sensed in a particular way, at a particular level of coarseness/granularity. This means that there is a disjunct between the movement patterns in the unobserved Universe and the movement patterns that are sensed. Following a visual sensing, a speck of thought/awareness conceptually moulds that which has been visually sensed. Through this process, the movements of feelings appear as objects – the parts that constitute an observed Universe.

In short, the Universal Feeling Body – the unobserved Universe – is a giant borderless movement pattern that is given the overwhelming majority of its movement by feelings feeling feelings. We can call this giant borderless movement pattern 'the intermediary', and it can be carved up in a ginormous number of ways. One could carve up very small segments of the intermediary – tiny movement patterns; or, one could carve up very large segments of the intermediary – massive movement patterns. Such vastly different carving is possible. In theory, a visual sense could be structured so as to sense just entities at the scale of atoms, or it could be structured so as to sense just entities at the scale of solar systems. However, as we have already explored, all of the visual sensory systems that have evolved in animal bodies on the Earth are medium-grained sensors.

Within the realm of medium-grained sensing there is a very wide range of granularity in terms of the scale of the movement patterns that are visually sensed, that are latched onto. And, this differential visual sensing of the intermediary provides a *range of possibility* for a speck to be able to conceptually mould possible parts. So, if the visual sense of a non-human animal body latches onto the smallest of the medium-grained sensing movement patterns, then it would be impossible for its speck to conceptually mould these patterns into parts such as 'cats', 'humans', 'trees', 'sausages', 'seagulls', and 'cars'. The sensed movement patterns are too small to allow this; these parts are outside its *range of possibility.* Where this non-human animal body visually senses movement, a human body will often, inevitably, sense non-movement.

The motionless observed Universe

It is hard for me to be certain that you have yet grasped the essential importance, the pivotal significance, of movement patterns. So, let us explore a thought experiment. Imagine that your observed Universe has no movements, and has never had any movements. Imagine that all of your knowledge comes from your observations of this Universe; there are no books to read, there are no databases to access, and there are no other sources of knowledge. What you are attempting to imagine is a motionless observed Universe. Let us be clear what this means. You are a speck of thought/awareness and nothing that you observe around you ever moves. So, you observe what appears to be a human body, but you don't have a conception that this is *your* body, because it never moves and it appears to be melded into its surroundings.

> *What usually gives rise to the conception that a speck of thought/awareness has an animal body is that this body stays a constant travelling companion through a changing kaleidoscope of background scenes.*

In our thought experiment, as none of the components of the human body move, and nothing else surrounding the body moves, one has no conception that the body has different limbs which do different things. One has no conception that the fingers on a hand can grasp things; one has no conception that knees can bend due to having kneecaps; one has no conception that toes can wiggle and that feet can walk; and, one has no conception that a neck can nod and shake.

As the human body and nothing that surrounds this body ever moves, one cannot meaningfully distinguish the body from its surroundings. Is the chair that surrounds most of the body part of the body? Does the body have angel wings, and a long tail, or is it wearing a fancy dress costume? There is no way of answering these questions. More than this, you wouldn't even have a conception of a human body, or what such an entity could possibly be! In our thought experiment, let us imagine that you observe in your surroundings what I, and no doubt you, would call: 'a cloud', 'a cow', 'a car', 'a caterpillar', 'a cat', 'a cabbage', 'a carrot', 'a chair', 'a carousel', 'a chip', 'a clock', 'a candle', and 'a cake'. These are parts, boundaried entities in our observed Universes, yet in our thought experiment, due to the lack of any movement, one cannot meaningfully distinguish these entities as distinct objects.

What is our conclusion? In the motionless observed Universe there are no distinct objects; there are no parts. To have a conceptual moulding, to have a conception of a part, a conception of a distinct entity, is typically to have a conception of how that thing moves against the backdrop of its surroundings. However, in some cases, to have a conception of a part is to have a conception of how *other* parts typically move in respect to this part. Let us flesh all of this out with some examples.

The origination of concepts in movement patterns

Our question to explore here is: How do concepts arise? One's concepts, one's conceptual mouldings, typically arise through putting a boundary around a particular movement pattern. For instance, when one's human body visually senses the movement pattern that is 'a butterfly flying', one can then conceptualise a butterfly as a distinct object, and it becomes a part in one's observed Universe. Similarly, when one's human body visually senses the movement pattern that is 'clouds drifting through the sky', one can then conceptualise a cloud and get a handle on what such an entity is. And, when one's human body visually senses the movement pattern that is 'a flag blowing in the wind', one can then make sense of what a flag is and can conceptually mould the flag into a part. Similarly, when one's human body visually senses the movement pattern that is 'a seagull flying', one can then put a boundary around this movement and conceptualise it as a 'seagull'; furthermore, whenever one encounters this movement pattern again one can easily re-establish the boundary of 'seagull' within one's observed Universe. When these parts have been delineated from their surroundings through their respective movement patterns, then one can typically quite easily identify them – a 'butterfly', a 'cloud', a 'flag', and a 'seagull' – when they are not moving. *For, one has knowledge of how these parts can move.*

In a similar vein, when one visually senses the movement pattern that is 'a pendulum swinging', one can then bring into being a boundary in one's observed Universe and establish the concept of a 'pendulum'. The same thing happens with a clock, or a watch; in the absence of the movement pattern that is hands moving around a clock face, or numbers moving on a screen, one would not mould these segments of the Universe into timepieces. Helicopters. Unless one has seen the movement pattern that is 'helicopter blades rotating', one will have no conception of what a helicopter is. Similarly, if one has not seen a car moving, then one will not mould cars as distinct boundaried objects within one's observed Universe. *The way that a helicopter moves is what it is. The way that a car moves is what it is.*

Let us imagine that a speck of thought/awareness has never ever seen a moving car, but then encounters a static car for the first time. The speck is presented with a visual sensing of non-movement. The speck will, no doubt, be curious. What is this segment of the Universe? Can it move? Can it move upwards and fly through the sky? Can it move downwards through the sea, like a 'submarine'? Can it spin like a carousel? Or, is it a statue? Is it separated from its surroundings? Are there lots of objects here, or is it one object, or is it part of a larger object? In the absence of movement, there are no answers. In the absence of movement, there is no car. However, if one visually senses the car moving, as it is driven, then there are no questions! The sensing of this movement pattern leads to a speck conceptually moulding the concept of a 'car'.

One's concepts, one's moulding of parts in one's observed Universe, can arise from observing how parts that have been moulded move in respect to a segment of the Universe. So, if one observes the movement pattern that is a 'human body' using a 'knife' to cut a segment of the Universe into slices, and then putting one of these slices into its 'mouth', one can then develop the concept of a 'cake'. A 'cake' is the movement pattern that is visually sensed that involves a segment of the Universe being cut and eaten. If one was in the motionless observed Universe, then one would never sense any movements concerning this segment of the Universe; one would not boundary it, conceptualise it, and take it to be a distinct part; one would have no 'cake' concept. Of course, there is an intertwining here; for the movements that other parts make in relation to an entity typically involve movements of that entity: the baker bakes the entity – the cake is created; the shopkeeper puts the entity on display – the cake moves; the cake is purchased and taken home – the cake moves; the cake is put on a table and sliced – the cake moves; the cake is handed around and put into mouths – the cake moves.

Of course, it is possible to develop a concept – generate a part – without the segment of the Universe in question ever appearing to move, due to how other parts are observed moving in relation to this segment. So, if one perceives a continuous flow of cars moving along a narrow segment of the Universe, one can then develop the concept of a 'road'. And, if one perceives several human bodies looking at a tiny segment of the Universe, whilst adjusting their hair, applying makeup, and shaving, then one can develop the concept of a 'mirror'. One could also get these two concepts in a very different way, by looking at a 'rear-view mirror' and thereby coming to appreciate that one is indirectly perceiving other moving vehicles, whilst one's human body is driving a car on a 'road'.

Differential visual sensings of the perpetually moving blank canvas

Let us remind ourselves that there is a disjunct between the movement patterns that are visually sensed and the movement patterns that exist in the unobserved Universe. The most important point to appreciate is that the observed Universe of parts that is forged by a speck is grounded in the level of granularity of the visual sensings that it is presented with. In other words, the types of movement pattern that are presented to a speck are determined by the structure of the visual sensory apparatus of its animal body. When movement is visually sensed, what is sensed is movement in a segment of the Universe, but the movement in this segment could be visually sensed in a plethora of different ways, as a plethora of different movement patterns. The unobserved Universe itself is simply one giant movement pattern – a fuzzy intermingling matrix of moving and radiating nodes of feeling.

The one giant movement pattern that is the unobserved Universe has a rich variety of different movement patterns within itself. One of these movement patterns brings into being a speck of thought/awareness. Yet, the unobserved Universe is like a perpetually moving blank canvas which, when it is observed, can be carved up, probed, latched onto, in a highly intricate way, from a zoomed out perspective, or from a great number of intermediate viewpoints. Nevertheless, despite the disjunct, there is a correlation between the movement patterns that are visually sensed and the movement patterns that exist in the unobserved Universe.

"I observe a helicopter"

Let us consider the movement pattern that in my observed Universe I perceive as: 'helicopter blades rotating'. What exactly is this movement? One could envision a helicopter that is on the surface of the Earth which has rotating blades. However, the term 'helicopter blades rotating' is actually shorthand for: 'helicopter blades rotating on a helicopter that is flying through the sky'. For, in my observed Universe, a 'helicopter' is a particular type of movement through the sky, and 'helicopter blades rotating' is this movement pattern. This conceptually moulded pattern is one viewpoint on the actual movement pattern that exists in this portion of the unobserved Universe.

In the unobserved Universe, the movement pattern that can be visually sensed and conceptually moulded as 'helicopter blades rotating' either exists or it does not exist. Whereas, in the observed Universe, when I assert that "I observe a helicopter", this can be in two scenarios.

Firstly, I can visually perceive the movement pattern that is 'helicopter blades rotating'. In this case, my visual sensing and conceptual moulding corresponds to a movement pattern that actually exists at that moment in time in the unobserved Universe.

Secondly, I can be visually perceiving a segment of the Universe which appears to be not moving, but which very closely resembles a segment of the Universe that I have observed moving in a particular way in the past ('helicopter blades rotating'). In this case, when I assert "I observe a helicopter", my inner process is effectively: *I believe that this segment of the Universe has the potential to bring into being the movement pattern that is 'helicopter blades rotating'; therefore, even though this segment is not moving at the moment I will boundary it, conceptually mould it as a part, as a distinct object: a 'helicopter'.*

In the observed Universe of parts, it is movement patterns that cause a speck of thought/awareness to create conceptual boundaries within the whole. In other words, in the observed Universe, parts are delineated by how they move; that is to say, parts are what they do. Whilst, in the unobserved Universe there are no parts, there are just the movements of the perpetually moving blank canvas.

The three levels of feeling and the glorious zenith

Recall that the diverse movement patterns that exist correspond to nodes and modes: the three levels of feeling nodes within the Universal Feeling Body, and the three modes of the Universe. In other words, the segments of the Universe that are inanimate are nodes of low-level feeling that move in a distinctive way, as compared to the movement patterns of nodes of medium-level feeling / that which is living without thought/awareness. Furthermore, all of these segments of the Universe move in a way that is distinctive from the movement patterns of that which is living with thought/awareness / is nodes of high-level feeling.

As the *Stages of Universal Unfoldment* progress, new movement patterns – patterns that are more complex and that feel more intensely – are joyously brought into existence. The movement patterns of technology correspond to the coming into being of high intensity feelings in animal bodies, particularly in human bodies. For, both the bringing forth and the utilisation of technology entails human bodies maximally actualising their potentials. These feelings and movements come into existence when the *Stages of Universal Unfoldment* are approaching their glorious zenith.

The kangaroo, the pogo stick, and the Chusan palm tree

Let us just say a little more on the subject of movement patterns! Let's think about a kangaroo. If you were in the motionless observed Universe you would not have a clue what a kangaroo is. In order to know what a kangaroo is, all that you need to do is to observe its magnificent movements. This movement pattern is what a kangaroo is! When you have observed the enormous jumps, then you know what a kangaroo is.

Imagine a pogo stick and a Chusan palm tree. I have selected these two parts in my observed Universe because they can conceivably very closely resemble each other. One can easily imagine a pogo stick that is designed to appear like a Chusan palm tree. And one can easily imagine a Chusan palm tree that resembles this pogo stick; for, the pogo stick has been designed to look like a Chusan palm tree! So, we have two parts which visually very closely resemble each other, but which are actually very different in terms of their nodes of feeling, their movement patterns, and their potential movement patterns. We are envisioning these two parts.

I strive to accurately conceptually mould that which my human body visually senses. If I have, in the past, conceptually moulded the two parts that we are envisioning, then when my human body visually senses what I take to be one of these parts I will initially conceptually mould it as both parts. In order to try and get to grips with what is being visually sensed I need to observe movement patterns. If I observe a human body standing on the entity and I see it springing off the surface of the Earth, lurching upwards, returning to the ground, only to lurch upwards once more; lurch and return; lurch and return; then, I will conclude: *that object is not a Chusan palm tree; it is a pogo stick!* I will boundary the movement, and I will confidently conceptually mould a particular part. In contrast, if the only movement patterns that I observe the entity making are, what appear to be leaves swaying in the wind, then I am likely to conclude: *this object is not a pogo stick; it is a Chusan palm tree!* I could be wrong; perhaps, if I had patiently observed for a lot longer, then I would have observed different movement patterns – lurching and returning.

The important point is that in the absence of any movement one cannot accurately distinguish these two parts. Lack of movement means that what one conceptually moulds, might not correspond to what is there. In the absence of springing, lurching, and returning, one could easily believe that the pogo stick is a living entity: a Chusan palm tree. Furthermore, one could come to believe that the Chusan palm tree is actually a pogo stick! Imagine that you are visually perceiving a particular segment of the Universe – our Chusan palm tree that resembles a pogo stick – you could imagine that if you stood on this part that you would joyously bounce off the surface of the Earth, as the object detached itself from the surface and propelled one upwards away from the ground. How disappointed one would be, when one came to realise that one was standing on a tree.

The movement of feeling versus the radiation of feeling

When one beholds the movements of feeling within the boundaryless entity that is the Universal Feeling Body, one will appreciate that there are vast differences in the speeds with which feelings move. Some exceptionally fast-moving feelings are what humans call: electricity, lightning strikes, and sunlight. Some slow-moving feelings are what humans call: worms, smells, snails, tortoises, dolphins, waterfalls, plants, grains of sand, bicycles, and humans. In between these extremes, we have moving feelings such as those that humans call: Concorde, music, space shuttles, and intercontinental ballistic missiles.

The immensely different speeds with which of nodes of feeling move — the sluggish diffusion of a smell, versus the galloping charge of sunlight, is a very different phenomenon from the instant radiation of feeling throughout a thing. For, feeling is continuously instantly radiating from every node of feeling within the Universal Feeling Body, irrespective of how fast that node of feeling is moving within the Universal Feeling Body.

Usain Bolt and the couch potato

Of course, as a speck of thought/awareness that is situated within a human body, one has the ability to choose how that body moves within one's Universal Feeling Body. One could choose to go hell for leather like Usain Bolt on a racetrack, or one could choose to mindfully walk like a Buddhist monk. One could choose to dance like a ballerina, to flow like a yogi, or to be a couch potato. One could choose to listen to the birds chirping and stop to smell the flowers, or one could choose to cover one's ears with headphones and block oneself off from the world.

However one chooses to move, it is very important for one to pay careful attention to the feelings that are forged as the feelings that are one's human body interact with the feelings that surround that body. For, it is this awareness that enables one to steer and guide one's human body onto its optimal trajectory towards health, wellbeing, and flourishing.

The falling tree and the primacy of 'secondary qualities'

Let us consider the part in my observed Universe that I call a 'tree'. If a tree falls in a forest, this is a movement within the Universal Feeling

Body. An immense plethora of new feelings are forged as the tree hits the ground. If these feelings were located in the legs or arms of a human body, its speck of thought/awareness might become aware of what it calls a 'bodily sensation'. If such feelings were on the tongue of a human whilst ingesting, its speck of thought/awareness might become aware of what it calls a 'taste'. If such feelings were in the nose of a human, its speck of thought/awareness might become aware of what it calls a 'smell'. If such feelings were sensed by the ear of a human, its speck of thought/awareness might become aware of what it calls a 'sound'.

Another way of putting this is to say that the Universe is pervaded with what are sometimes called 'secondary qualities': feelings = tastes = smells = sounds. Of course, this label is not very suitable; indeed, it is highly inappropriate. For, these qualities pervade the Universe and they have an observer-independent existence, a speck-independent existence. These qualities are the fundamental nature of the Universe; there is nothing 'secondary' about them! If a tree falls in a forest, this segment of the Universe is pervaded with new feelings = tastes = smells = sounds.

The unobserved Universe contains qualities such as motion, extension, duration, position, and size, but these qualities are not 'primary'; for, these qualities are grounded in the interactions of nodes of feeling. Furthermore, the way that these qualities appear to a particular speck, in its observed Universe of parts, is dependent on the structured visual sensing of its animal body. For, as we have explored, in the unobserved Universe these qualities are fuzzy. So, 'secondary qualities' are primary. More precisely, feelings are primary.

The primacy of feeling over thought

A speck of thought/awareness and feeling can interact in various ways. In considering these interactions, a useful phrase to keep in mind is: 'the primacy of feeling over thought'. This phrase comes into play when there is a clash between feeling quality and thought content. Often there is no such clash. If a speck of thought/awareness has the thought content: 'this human is beautiful', whilst simultaneously becoming aware of feelings of attraction that arise in its animal body whilst in the company of the human in question, then there is no thought/feeling clash. Rather, there is concordance between feeling quality and thought content.

There need not be such concordance. Feelings of attraction in an animal body can be accompanied by an opposing thought content: 'this human is unattractive'. Here there is a clash between feeling quality and thought content and this means that 'the primacy of feeling over thought' comes into play. The truth, the reality of the situation, resides in the feeling state. The thought is a falsehood. The feeling states that come into being – the feeling states which radiate out from the speck's animal body – are feelings of attraction. It matters not a jot that the speck has the thought: 'this human is unattractive'. The reality, as revealed by their feeling states, is that they find the human to be attractive.

Non-human animals

It is fruitful to consider 'the primacy of feeling over thought' when it comes to the way that non-human animals interact with humans. The movement patterns of nodes of feeling that are the bodies of non-human animals, when they encounter a human body, will feel the human body by 'tuning in' to the feelings that are the human body. This is very easily achieved; for, the human body, as an epicentre of high-level feelings, will be a dominant component of the world of pure feeling that is inhabited by the nodes of feeling of the non-human animal body. The issue at stake is: Does this human body radiate feelings of love and compassion? Or, does it radiate feelings of hatred and aggression? Is the human body friend or foe? Is it a danger? A hunter? A killer of animals? This 'tuning in', this episode of feelings feeling feelings, concerns the feelings that constitute the human body, the feelings that the human body radiates.

In the scenario that we are considering, it matters not a jot what the thought content of the speck in the human body is. A human body can have feelings of love and compassion towards a non-human animal, whist its speck of thought/awareness simultaneously has the thought content: 'I don't like you and am going to eat you for breakfast'. This thought content clearly does not describe the reality of the situation. The thought content can be a purely non-serious thing, a moment of internal joviality. The true/real intentions, of the human are revealed not by the thought content of their speck, but by the feelings in their human body. 'The primacy of feeling over thought' is a universal truth.

The primacy of feeling over speech: the 'creepy' human

Another perspective to consider is how the speck of thought/awareness in a human body assesses another human. If one encounters another human and is 'creeped out' by them, if one becomes aware of a feeling of impending doom, and imminent danger, then it matters not a jot that this 'creepy' human then utters the words: 'I really like you and want to help you'. In the face of such words being uttered one would be sensible to adopt the approach of: 'the primacy of feeling over speech', and act accordingly. Such an approach could be rephrased as: 'the primacy of feeling over auditory outputs'. This is the primacy of the feelings that one becomes aware of, over the words that one hears.

Of course, there is more to be said about the scenario that we have just considered. For, we earlier explored the distinction that exists between the feeling content of uttered words, and the actual words themselves. When it comes to one's encounter with the human that results in one being 'creeped out', one became aware of the high intensity feelings that are originating in the 'creepy' human's body (in the absence of them speaking). However, when this 'creepy' human speaks then one is also likely to detect that one is in danger due to the feeling content of their uttered words. It matters not a jot what the actual words are.

The disjunct between thought and speech

There can, of course, also be a disjunct between thought and speech: a speck of thought/awareness can think something and the voice of its human body can say the opposite. We are talking about simple deceit and manipulation; or, hiding the truth in the hope of doing the right thing. However, our interest is simply in the various disjuncts that occur between feeling content and spoken words, and between feeling content and thoughts. In this respect, the key thing to keep in mind is always 'the primacy of feeling': the primacy of feeling over thought content, and the primacy of feeling over speech content.

Reality is described by feelings, not by thoughts/words

None of that which we have recently been exploring will be a surprise to you. If you have a pet that you love, that you absolutely adore, you know that you can be full of feelings of love and compassion for your pet, whilst simultaneously having this thought about your pet, or uttering these words to your pet: 'I don't like you and am going to eat you for breakfast'. Reality is described by feelings, not by thoughts/words. Here the word 'reality' is used in two different ways. Firstly, the truth of a particular situation: in this scenario, the true intentions towards one's pet. Such intentions are not derivable from thoughts/words. Secondly, describing the fundamental nature of the Universe: the Universal Feeling Body. These two descriptions are simply referring to two very different spatial scales: the microcosm and the macrocosm.

Tiny barges

The Universal Feeling Body – the unobserved Universe – is an ocean of perennially flowing feeling, which in certain places and at certain times brings forth specks of thought/awareness. Envision tiny barges bobbing up and down on a stormy ocean. The ocean is a web of flowing feeling; the barges are its specks of thought/awareness. The truth, the power, the energy, the reality, the vitality, lies within the stormy ocean, not within the tiny barges.

 # The primacy of feeling in spoken words: the broken human, 'I am going to come and get you', and undecipherable gobbledegook

A little more can fruitfully be said concerning the relationship between words that are spoken and the feeling content of these words. Spoken words are feelings. Spoken words are a projection, an emanation, of the feeling state of the speaker. This feeling state might be in accordance with the actual words that are spoken. However, it might not be in such accordance. A human can say: "I am ecstatically happy. I am amazing. I am thriving. I am on cloud nine. The world is my oyster". Yet, the feeling state of these words can reveal that they are terribly depressed, broken, miserable, and in a hopeless state of gloom and despair.

A string of uttered words such as: 'I am going to come and get you', says nothing about the reality of the situation. These words can be spoken with feelings of compassion and care. They can be spoken with feelings of lust. They can be spoken with feelings of condescension. They can be spoken with feelings of hostility/aggression. The feeling content of these spoken words could be the feelings of love of a concerned parent who is assuring their stranded child that they will help them. The feeling content of these spoken words could be the feelings of rage of a stranger who is holding a knife in a dark alley.

If one wants to assess a human's intentions one assesses the way that their words are spoken. What is the tone of their voice? How are their words spoken? In other words, what feelings are emanating from them via their spoken words? The words themselves, the string of letters, are of no use in assessing a human's intentions. What matters is the feeling content of the spoken words. The feeling content of the spoken word always trumps the words themselves.

Of course, if one does not understand the language that words are being spoken in, then, when one's human body auditorily senses the feelings that are spoken words, one will not create an auditory output such as: 'I am going to come and get you'. One's auditory output will simply be: 'undecipherable gobbledegook'. In this case, all that one has to go on is the feeling content of that which has been uttered.

Feeling and body language

You are surely familiar with the view of human communication that I am about to outline and discuss. According to this view, when a human seeks to understand what another human is communicating when they utter words, the words themselves only account for a trivial 7% of their interpretation. A comparatively massive 38% of the interpreted meaning of what a human is communicating comes from the manner in which the words are vocalised. In other words, 38% of the meaning comes from the feeling content of the spoken words. We have already explored this primacy of feeling in determining the meaning of spoken words.

We haven't yet explored the remaining 55% of the interpreted meaning of spoken words. This meaning comes from the speaker's body language: gestures, facial expressions, and all of their other bodily movements. We have already explored the connection between movement and feeling. Any movement involves, generates, a change in feeling. More than this, throughout the Universal Feeling Body, feelings – feelings feeling feelings – are the drivers of movements.

What about specks of thought/awareness? As we have already explored, whilst specks can initiate movements, these movements are ultimately grounded in the realm of feeling. This means that feelings are the drivers of body language. The gestures, facial expressions, and all of the other movements of animal bodies, both reveal the present feeling state of the animal body, and forge its future feeling state.

What this means is that an enormous 93% of the interpreted meaning of what a human is communicating when they speak comes from the realm of their feeling state – a state which is revealed by their body language (55%) and by the feeling content of their words (38%). The meaning has almost nothing to do with words, and almost everything to do with feeling. In the Universal Feeling Body, in the Universe, feelings are 'king'.

The aspects of the Universal Feeling Body, and the categorisation of parts

The Universal Feeling Body is far from homogenous. Bits of it are nodes of high-level feeling; bits of it are nodes of medium-level feeling; bits of it are nodes of low-level feeling. Bits of it are sites of deeply embedded feeling; bits of it are sites of scattered feeling. Bits of it are sites of rapidly changing/flowing feeling; bits of it are sites of relatively static feeling. It is inevitable that your human body will feel drawn to, and be invigorated by, certain aspects of the Universal Feeling Body.

Despite having all of these aspects, the Universal Feeling Body is a single borderless whole. A lack of borders and homogeneity are two very different beasts. Within the single borderless whole, in the year 2024, there are three distinctive movement patterns. That which originates low-level feeling – collections of nodes of low-level feeling – has a very distinctive type of movement within the single borderless whole. That which originates medium-level feeling – collections of nodes of medium-level feeling – has a very distinctive type of movement within the single borderless whole. And, of course, that which originates high-level feeling – collections of nodes of high-level feeling – also has a very distinctive type of movement within the single borderless whole.

It is very important to appreciate that the *different levels of feeling / distinctive movement patterns* directly map onto the three modes of the Universe. Our question is: Why does this mapping occur? Our answer: Universal Unfoldment. As the Universe has unfolded through the *Stages of Universal Unfoldment,* it has been propelled by the process of feelings feeling feelings. This process inevitably entails the bringing into being of movement patterns that progressively feel more intensely; for, such intensity is desirable, sought after, and grabbed onto. And, these diverse feelings / movement patterns directly map onto the three modes via the two min-chasms that are unfolded — the three modes of the Universe that are inanimate, living without thought/awareness, and living with thought/awareness.

There is another crucial aspect to this that that requires consideration: the nature of the relationship between the unobserved Universe and the observed Universe. The mapping between feelings/patterns/modes that we have just explored occurs in the unobserved Universe — the Universal Feeling Body. When we switch our attention to an observed Universe of parts, then we can see that the distinctive feelings/patterns/modes that exist in the unobserved Universe will very closely match the conceptual mouldings of a speck of thought/awareness. Our question here is: Why does this matching occur? Our answer: such matching occurs because the visual sense of an animal body senses medium-grained movement patterns, and then its speck conceptually moulds distinctive movement patterns into particular parts. Furthermore, and crucially, the three distinctive types of movement pattern in the unobserved Universe are visually sensed, through a structured visual sensing, as three distinctive types of movement pattern. A consequence of this is that when these distinctive movement patterns are conceptually moulded into particular parts by a speck, it naturally categorises its parts into three groups according to the similarities of the respective movement patterns. And, these three groups will be the three modes of the Universe. So, *low-level feelings / movement patterns / Mode 1 bits of the Universal Feeling Body* are typically conceptually moulded as being inanimate ('non-living') by a speck. *Medium-level feelings / movement patterns / Mode 2 bits of the Universal Feeling Body* are typically conceptually moulded as that which is living without thought/awareness ('plant'/'fungi') by a speck. And, *high-level feelings / movement patterns / Mode 3 bits of the Universal Feeling Body* are typically conceptually moulded by a speck to be that which is living with thought/awareness ('animal'). I have used the word 'typically' because misidentifications, incorrect categorisations can occur. For instance, a speck of thought/awareness could conceptually mould a particular bit of the Universal Feeling Body as *medium-level feelings / movement patterns / Mode 2 bits of the Universal Feeling Body;* yet, in reality, what exists in this bit of the Universal Feeling Body is *low-level feelings / movement patterns / Mode 1 bits of the Universal Feeling Body.* This misidentification can occur when the segment of the Universe in question is a plastic plant that moves like a real plant; it can also occur when a pogo stick is conceptually moulded as a Chusan palm tree.

When a speck is categorising its conceptually moulded parts into these three groups it need not be fully cognisant of what it is doing. So, one could ask the specks that are located in two human bodies this question: Do you believe that a cow has a speck of thought/awareness? And, one could get two different answers: a 'yes' and a 'no'. Yet, despite this, both of these specks will categorise that segment of the Universe that the visual sense of their animal body senses as moving in a particular way, and which they conceptually mould as a 'cow', as being a Mode 3 segment of the Universe (that which lives with thought/awareness). So, the categorisation will be correct, even if a speck has a false belief (the belief: 'a cow does not have a speck of thought/awareness').

Appreciating one's Universal Feeling Body

One can become aware that one has a Universal Feeling Body; one can become aware that one is a speck of thought/awareness that is guided by the feelings of the Universe; one can become aware that everything that one visually perceives is a state of feeling: feeling feeling feeling. The question before us is: When one reaches this level of insight is this likely to change the way that one lives one's life? Our answer is: Yes; such a level of insight will affect one in a number of ways.

Firstly, one will take more interest in one's surroundings, will dwell in them, ponder them, appreciate them, and rejoice in them. In this way, one is simply paying attention to one's Universal Feeling Body. Also, that which is alive will appear more vibrant and vivid.

Secondly, one will become increasingly aware of the plethora of ways in which one's own feelings and actions affect the feelings that other specks become aware of, thereby potentially causing them to be 'in pain' and to suffer. This increasing awareness is likely to lead one to live a kinder life.

Thirdly, one will become increasingly aware of the feelings that one is deeply embedded with, and will consequently become increasingly knowledgeable concerning the places/activities that bolster one's human body and the places/activities that drag it down. In this way, one can improve one's steering of one's animal body so that it lives its best life and maximises its potential.

Fourthly, one will become increasingly aware of situations in which one almost certainly seems to have become aware of feelings that originated outside of one's animal body. These situations might well involve other animal bodies and their high intensity feelings, such as extreme pain, fear, desperation, exhilaration, and elation. However, at a broader level, one will come to appreciate that everything that one hears are feelings, the vast majority of which originate outside of one's animal body.

Fifthly, one will pay increasing consideration to the nodes of feeling that one ingests and digests: Is it pain? Is it suffering? How pure are the feelings and the feeling memories? How does ingesting and digesting particular types of nodes of feeling make one's animal body feel?

Finally, one will increasingly consider one's surroundings. Is one's home dominated by deeply embedded feelings or by scattered feelings? What is the nature of these feelings? Would one's human body benefit from having medium-level feelings (such as houseplants) or high-level feelings (pets or other human bodies) in one's home? Does one's human body wear second-hand clothes? If it does, what is the nature of the feeling memories that are these clothes? Does one become aware of a greater sense of wellbeing when one's human body is surrounded by high-level feelings, or medium-level feelings, or low-level feelings? Does one's human body feel at ease in an inland city (deeply embedded feeling) or in a small village that is located by the seaside (scattered feeling)? Or, does it need a balance between deeply embedded feeling and scattered feeling? If so, then it might thrive in a city that is located on the coast.

The magical beauty of visual perception

When one fully appreciates that what one visually perceives is created by one, then what one visually perceives becomes almost magical to one. One realises that what one visually perceives is fundamentally part of one. Without one, what one visually perceives would not exist. One is bringing this magical beauty into existence.

This is, seemingly, something that needs to be experienced in order to be understood. The magical beauty of visual perception cannot be adequately conveyed through words.

Dwelling in one's experiences

One can have an intellectual grasp of the Universal Feeling Body without getting to know the Universal Feeling Body. The aim of this book is to provide you with the tools that enable you to be able to intellectually grasp the Universal Feeling Body. The hard work then begins. When you have the intellectual grasp, you then have the opportunity to dwell in your experiences and to let the Universal Feeling Body be your guide.

You can just observe and ponder. This is harder than it sounds. Observe the way that you behold the movements that surround you, come to appreciate that these movements are your body, and ponder how you instinctively carve them up into parts. The distinctive movements of the squirrels, the birds, the humans, the rabbits, the dogs, the frogs, the dragonflies, the fish, the bees, and the deer – these movements are the zenith of the *Stages of Universal Unfoldment;* these are the movements of that which has a speck of thought/awareness. The rustling of the leaves of the trees, the swaying of the flowers; when you boundary these movements you know that you are boundarying that bit of your Universal Feeling Body that is living without thought/awareness. Observe and ponder. Come to know that what you are observing is created by you. There are no parts without you. Without you there are just the movements of the feeling whole and its tiny barges; movements that become more joyous, and magical, and exuberant, as the *Stages of Universal Unfoldment* approach their glorious zenith.

The birds, the spiders, the butterflies, the seahorses, the helicopters, the trees; these are not parts that are opposed to you. These segments of the Universe are bits of your body, bits of your Universal Feeling Body. All of the feelings that you become aware of, including all of the sounds that you hear, are feelings that are located in your Universal Feeling Body. You are a tiny barge that is floating upon an immense ocean of feeling.

I have a beautiful body

That which I visually perceive is my body. Everything that I visually perceive is my body. Everything that I visually perceive is my Universal Feeling Body. What a beautiful body I have!

Perhaps you still believe that you only have an animal body. Let me try and communicate what it means to experience one's Universal Feeling Body, by comparing it to one's experiences of one's animal body.

The rustling of the leaves of the trees are tingling sensations in one's fingers and toes. The water that flows through streams, evaporates, transpires, and falls from clouds, is blood joyously circulating around one's veins. Rays of sunshine are glowing feelings that overwhelm one's body. The screams of agony in the war zone are pains in one's chest. The clouds floating through the sky are moments of bliss. The chirps of the birds are tickles in one's torso. Earthquakes are rancid rumblings in one's stomach. Hurricanes and tornadoes are one's body being viciously mauled in a boxing ring. Lightning strikes are shooting pains in one's nerves. And the orbiting of the planets around the Sun, and the Moon around the Earth, are one's changing moods.

Creating the future

We recently explored the various ways in which an appreciation of the existence of the Universal Feeling Body might lead you to live your life a little differently. If enough humans come to know the Universal Feeling Body, such an appreciation might even help to usher in a more peaceful world, a world in which feelings of pain and suffering are reduced. This outcome would come about due to both the way in which specks relate to the human bodies in which they are situated, and the way that they relate to their Universal Feeling Body.

Envisioning your Universal Feeling Body and exploring your human body

Can you envision your beautiful Universal Feeling Body? Have you come to appreciate that your human body is an epicentre of high-level feelings, and that feelings are continuously moving and radiating into this body, flowing within it, and that as feelings exit your human body they excite your Universal Feeling Body? You are a speck of thought/awareness, but this does not say that much about you; for, the 'I' that is you is a qualityless window.

To discover the uniqueness of your human body you need to explore it; for, it is a unique segment of the Universe. It is here that your feelings will be your guide, as you seek to discover, to become aware of, the particular skills, abilities, and aptitudes that your human body has. Your human body is constituted out of feelings, and these feelings enable you to steer and guide your human body so as to maximise its potential, to utilise its skills/abilities/aptitudes, and thereby to flourish. Your human body is a unique and immensely precious piece of the Universal Feeling Body. The only thing that is more precious is you.

Let your feelings be your guide and embrace both your human body and your Universal Feeling Body.

The concept of mind

Towards the beginning of our exploration into the Universal Feeling Body I claimed that if one wishes to give an account of everything that exists in the Universe that one has no need for the concept of 'mind'.

Now that we are nearing the end of our exploration I am happy to assert that wherever a speck of thought/awareness exists, that a 'mind' exists. Given our exploration into the Universal Feeling Body, I am hopeful that you will now have a clear idea of what this term really means, if you wish to use it. A 'mind' is simply a speck of thought/awareness. A 'mind' is a qualityless window which sits at the boundary between the observed Universe and the Universal Feeling Body.

A speck of thought/awareness – a 'mind' – intermittently emerges in an animal brain. Irrespective of whether or not a speck exists, this brain will be engaged in computation, because a brain is a computation device. Computation itself does not entail the existence of a mind. Complex arrangements of the non-living can engage in computation without ever giving rise to a speck of thought/awareness.

A speck of thought/awareness – a 'mind' – will become aware of the feelings in its Universal Feeling Body (tastes = smells = sounds = bodily sensations = touches = feelings), but such feelings do not entail the existence of a mind. For, such feelings exist in the complete absence of a speck of thought/awareness and they pervade the Universe.

A speck of thought/awareness – a 'mind' – will become aware of the sensings of the visual sense of its animal body (if the animal body has a visual sense), but such sensings do not entail the existence of a mind. For, visual sensings can exist in the complete absence of a speck. For instance, a robot can visually sense its surroundings, but it has no speck of thought/awareness, which means that it does not conceptually mould its visual sensings. A robot does not visually perceive its surroundings; it does not have an observed Universe of parts.

A speck of thought/awareness – a 'mind' – will become aware of the unique abilities/skills/aptitudes of its animal body, by becoming aware of both the movements of this body and the feelings which accompany these movements. However, abilities/skills/aptitudes do not entail the existence of a mind; for, they exist in the complete absence of a speck of thought/awareness; indeed, they pervade the Universe.

You surely know that all of this is true. For, you have come to know, to intimately befriend, both your animal body and your Universal Feeling Body; and, from such a vantage point, this is all blindingly apparent.

I am a speck of thought/awareness, therefore I am

I am a speck of thought/awareness, therefore I am.

I am nothing more than a speck of thought/awareness.

I am nothing less than a speck of thought/awareness.

The existence of a mind, the question of whether or not a mind exists, has nothing whatsoever to do with the existence of feelings = tastes = smells = sounds = bodily sensations. The existence of a mind has nothing whatsoever to do with the existence of visual sensings. The existence of a mind has nothing whatsoever to do with computation. The existence of a mind has nothing whatsoever to do with the abilities/skills/aptitudes of animal bodies. The existence of a mind is the existence of the qualityless window that is a speck of thought/awareness.

Two types of entities – specks and feelings

There are two very different types of entities that exist in the Universal Feeling Body: nodes of feeling and specks of thought/awareness. Feelings feel and feeling interactions thereby bring into being certain movement patterns in the Universal Feeling Body. These movement patterns can be visually sensed by a structured visual sensing, and then be conceptually moulded into parts. All of the parts that are conceptually moulded are movement patterns of feelings. A speck of thought/awareness emerges when a particular movement pattern of feelings exists.

A speck of thought/awareness is a very different entity to a feeling. A speck of thought/awareness is a qualityless window; it is a not a feeling entity. So, that which feels, when it moves in a certain way in the brain of an animal, brings forth that which does not feel. The purpose of this bringing forth is to enable the steering and guiding of the animal body so that it can positively flourish in the realm of high intensity feelings of attraction, whilst steering away from feelings of repulsion.

That which feels emerges that which does not feel

Do you find it strange, possibly even incoherent, that that which feels brings into existence an entity that does not feel? Do you find it strange that that which does not feel – a speck of thought/awareness – makes decisions which lead to changes in its Universal Feeling Body? That is to say, a speck makes decisions which either causes the feelings that are its human body to move in a particular way, or to not move, and both of these outcomes change its entire Universal Feeling Body. In this way, that which does not feel, that which is brought into existence by feelings feeling feelings, inevitably changes the feeling of feelings.

To be fair, you might very reasonably have found almost everything that has been written in this book to be strange; for, what has been written could very violently clash with beliefs that you have held ever since you were a small child. However, if one ponders the matter, one will surely realise that there is nothing particularly strange about that which feels arranging itself in a way which enables the bringing forth of an entity that does not feel. Whilst a speck is a non-feeling entity that is brought into existence by feelings, it does not exist in a different realm. It is firmly situated within the brain of an animal; it has no separate existence; it cannot float off and leave its brain; it is part of the functioning of a brain.

The 'brain activity' movement pattern and the 'speck of thought/awareness' movement pattern

The speck of thought/awareness that is intermittently brought into existence in an animal brain, when that brain has a particular movement pattern of feelings, is a non-feeling entity: a qualityless window. A speck of thought/awareness cannot be observed because it is located in the unobserved Universe. That which can be observed in the brain of an animal are the parts of one's observed Universe – the movements of feelings that one's human body has visually sensed in a structured way and that one has conceptually moulded.

Let us consider the entire brain of an animal. What does it mean to talk of a brain? What does it mean to isolate, to conceptually mould, to boundary, a particular segment of the Universe and label it as 'a brain'? The segments of the Universe that the specks of thought/awareness in human bodies conceptually mould as 'a brain' are a particular type of movement pattern within the Universal Feeling Body. And, you will recall that particular movement patterns do particular things. *That is to say, movement patterns are certain abilities/skills/aptitudes.* For instance, the movement pattern that is 'metabolism' brings life into existence. When this movement pattern was first brought forth in the Universal Feeling Body, then life had evolved in the Universe – a mini-chasm opened as Mode 1 transformed into Mode 2. Whilst, the movement pattern that is 'steam train rolling' transports humans and commodities across the surface of the Earth. And, the movement pattern that is 'sunlight' provides the energy that enables life to exist on the Earth.

The prime movement pattern that exists in the bits of the Universal Feeling Body where 'brains' can be visually perceived in an observed Universe – the 'brain activity' movement pattern – is the ability that is computation. The 'brain activity' movement pattern sits within a broader family of movement patterns – 'computation' movement patterns – which spans both the living and the non-living segments of the Universe. In those bits of the Universal Feeling Body where 'brains' can be visually perceived in an observed Universe, there sometimes exists another very important movement pattern; a movement pattern that is unique to these bits of the Universal Feeling Body; this is the movement pattern which corresponds to the existence of a speck of thought/awareness in the unobserved Universe.

Why a speck of thought/awareness has an intermittent existence

The Universal Feeling Body is one giant borderless movement pattern: a perpetually moving blank canvas, which is comprised of distinctive types of movements that are brought into being as feelings feel feelings, and specks of thought/awareness shepherd feelings. These distinctive movement patterns can be visually sensed by a structured visual sensing, and this act of visual sensing transmorphs a movement pattern into a different movement pattern.

Conceptually isolating tiny bits of the intermediary – a 'steam train rolling', a 'flower', a 'tree', a 'kangaroo', 'Totnes Castle', a 'human', 'butter', a 'fly', a 'butterfly', a 'fish', a 'thumb', a 'finger', a 'chocolate', a 'chocolate finger', a 'fish finger' – is a full-time endeavour for a speck of thought/awareness. This endeavour is an extremely tiring one, and this is why a speck has an intermittent existence; it needs to recharge its batteries, recuperate, and build up to the next onslaught of conceptual moulding and boundarying. Whilst it is extremely tiring, this onslaught is essential; it is required in order to enable a speck of thought/awareness to keep its animal body alive and safe.

General anaesthetics and sleep

We have seen that when a particular movement pattern of feelings exists in an animal brain, then a speck of thought/awareness exists. When this movement pattern does not exist, then a speck of thought/awareness does not exist. When this movement pattern does not exist, then the animal body could be in a state of sleep. Alternatively, the lack of this movement pattern could have another cause; for example, it could have been induced by drugs, such as general anaesthetics.

There are important differences between the state of sleep and the state of being under a general anaesthetic. For, drugs have multiple effects on an animal brain. Our interest is simply in the fact that the absence of the movement pattern of feelings in an animal brain that generates a speck of thought/awareness can be both a state of sleep and a drug-induced state. In such a state there is no 'I'; there is no entity that can be 'in pain' or suffer. Yet, feeling states of extreme repulsion – high intensity feelings – can still exist in the animal body; states that would cause a speck of thought/awareness to be 'in pain' if it existed in the animal body.

You might well think that all of this is obvious. However, it needs to be stated; for, the erroneous belief does exist that general anaesthetic eliminates the feeling of pain. The reality is that general anaesthetic eliminates the awareness of the feeling of pain; for, it inhibits the movement pattern that generates a speck of thought/awareness.

What is the movement pattern that generates a speck of thought/awareness?

A speck of thought/awareness comes into existence when a particular oscillation pattern exists in an animal brain.

What is instant radiation throughout a thing?

Can you clearly envision what it means to talk of the instant radiation of a feeling throughout a thing? It might be useful to compare the instant radiation of a feeling throughout a thing to a journey that is undertaken by your human body. You can imagine that your human body is currently in Exeter, but that you want to take it to Dawlish, Teignmouth, Newton Abbot, Totnes, Plymouth, Saltash, St Germans, and Liskeard. What a list of wonderful destinations! This aim can be achieved by getting on a train at Exeter St Davids which will stop at each of these places on its journey.

You can envision that each of these locations is a node of feeling that jointly constitutes a thing. What it means for a feeling to instantly radiate throughout this thing *is not* for it to move from Exeter to Dawlish, and then to Teignmouth, and then to Newton Abbot, and then to Totnes, and so on. If these locations constituted a thing, then as soon as the feeling originates in Exeter it is felt simultaneously in Plymouth, St Germans, Totnes, Liskeard, Saltash, Newton Abbot, Teignmouth, and Dawlish. So, we are not talking about a journey; rather, we are talking about a single instantaneous occurrence that is instantiated in discrete locations.

What is an observation?

An act of visual perception is an observation. Visual perception requires a speck of thought/awareness to conceptually mould that which has been visually sensed. Yet, as we have explored, perception without awareness is possible. When a speck has created a conceptual moulding, then visual perception can occur in its absence. Nevertheless, an observed Universe – a world of distinct parts – requires a speck of thought/awareness.

It will be fruitful to delve a little deeper into the realm of visual sensing, conceptual moulding, visual perception, and observation. Our question: Could visual sensing itself, in the total absence of a speck, be sufficient for there to be an observation? One could answer this question both 'no' and 'yes'. If by 'observation' one means the beholding of a part, of an object, then visual sensing is not sufficient for observation; for, parts are conceptual mouldings. However, if by 'observation' one just means a segment of the Universe registering data about another segment of the Universe, then visual sensing, such as that carried out by a robot, would be sufficient for there to be an observation. Furthermore, on this latter conceptualisation of 'observation', every node of feeling in the Universal Feeling Body would be forever observing in the world of pure feeling. So, perhaps, every segment of the Universe differentially observes all of the other segments of the Universe, giving us the Universal Observing Body.

Implications for physics

A speck of thought/awareness is influenced in various ways, in particular by the feelings of its Universal Feeling Body, but it ultimately determines itself. A speck of thought/awareness is free to decide what to do; it's decisions are not determined by that which is not itself; it could have chosen to do other than what it did. Our central question here is: Is this ability in conflict with the realm of physics? For, a physicist might want to assert that everything that occurs in a brain is determined by some fundamental laws which apply to the entire Universe, or at least to large segments of the Universe, segments that incorporate animal brains.

There is no conflict here, for the domain of physics is the realm of the observed Universe of parts; whilst, specks of thought/awareness and feelings exist in the unobserved Universe. Let us recall that visual sensing is a structured activity, structured by the particular makeup of the visual sensory system of a specific animal body. This structure causes an animal body to transmorph the fuzzy intermingling movement patterns that exist in the Universal Feeling Body into sensed movement patterns, and then its speck conceptually moulds this structured appearance into parts through establishing boundaries. This is the two-stage process of visual perception. Physics is imprisoned, inevitably forever constrained, by this process of structured visual sensing and conceptual moulding. So, the observable and unobservable entities that physics deals with – planets, apples, atoms, leptons, gluons, electrons, and the like – are entities that potentially exist for humans, are entities that are postulated to exist, due to the structured sensings of the human visual sense. These postulated parts arise due to the conceptual mouldings of structured transmorphing sensings by specks in human bodies. Such entities have no existence in the boundaryless realm that is the Universal Feeling Body!

The realm of physics is the realm of the feeling structures – the parts – that a speck has conceptually moulded; it is not the realm of nodes of feeling, things, and specks themselves. Within the Universal Feeling Body

– the unobserved Universe – there are no boundaries; it is a giant fuzzy borderless movement pattern: the perpetually moving blank canvas, which, as the *Stages of Universal Unfoldment* advance, in certain places, for brief periods of time, brings forth a floating tiny barge. When the intermediary is visually sensed and then conceptually moulded into an observed Universe of parts by a speck, specific movement patterns and apparent non-movement are carved/transmorphed out of the distinctive movements of the perpetually moving blank canvas. This process can incorporate the 'brain activity' movement pattern. That is to say, a brain can be a part in an observed Universe. Yet, this segment of the Universe is really just a particular type of movement that can be pointed towards within the larger movement pattern that is the Universal Moving Body.

The observed Universe that appears to a speck of thought/awareness is created by itself, so this observed Universe is inevitably intelligible to the speck. It could not possibly be unintelligible; for, it has been created precisely in order to make what has been visually sensed intelligible. Physics is an endeavour which is wholly located within the inevitably intelligible appearance that is created by physicists themselves. In other words, the physics that is carried out is inevitably in accordance with the observed Universe that the speck of thought/awareness in a physicist creates when it conceptually moulds its transmorphed structured visual sensings into particular parts.

Physics has nothing to say about specks of thought/awareness. Physics has nothing to say about the things that constitute the Universal Feeling Body. For, the fundamental nature of the Universe is not its domain. Its domain is the superficial observed Universe of parts that the specks of thought/awareness in physicists actively create. Such active creation is an absolute necessity as specks of thought/awareness incessantly strive to perceive a Universe that is intelligible.

Physics necessarily entails free will

You might have heard the idea that the laws of physics prohibit the existence of free will. Don't be persuaded by this idea. It is actually the case that without free will there would be no physics! For, the existence of a speck of thought/awareness is the existence of free will. And, the existence of a speck of thought/awareness is necessary if there is both to be an observed Universe of parts which can be experimented upon, and an experimenter who can do the experiments.

Without a speck of thought/awareness, without free will, there is no 'I'; there is no physicist. Without a speck of thought/awareness, without free will, there is no observed Universe of parts to be investigated.

> *The science of physics necessarily entails the existence of free will. That is to say, a speck of thought/awareness provides the possibility for physics to emerge in the observed Universe of parts that is created by a speck of thought/awareness.*

The exceptionally important gift

You have an exceptionally important gift. You have the ability to steer and guide your human body in order to enable it to flourish, to actualise its potential, and thereby to become an increasingly precious piece of the Universal Feeling Body.

Mystical environmental philosophy

I consider this to be a work of mystical philosophy. I very much hope that you have enjoyed reading it. Writing it has certainly been an adventure! As we draw to an end, we are at the beginning. For, that which is covered in this book provides the foundations for something which is much more profound: 'mystical environmental philosophy'. Mystical environmental philosophy is concerned with what it means to be human, the place of the human species within our unfolding Solar System, human cosmic purpose, and how all of these things are related to global warming and the 'environmental crisis' of modernity.

To cut a long story short, mystical environmental philosophy reveals why the human species is the most precious part of both our Solar System, and any solar system, and uncloaks the human species as the saviour of life on Earth. In the absence of the human species, life on Earth would be doomed. Life on Earth brought forth the human species into existence so that it could save itself. There is no doubt about this; there is no room for debate; this is an absolute certainty.

There are not that many absolute certainties. These things are absolute certainties:

'I am a speck of thought/awareness, therefore I am'

The external world exists

The unobserved Universe is the Universal Feeling Body

An observed Universe of parts is created by a speck of thought/awareness

Life exists

Life on Earth brought forth the human species into existence so that it could save itself

If you are interested in learning more about this, my book is: *Mystical Environmental Philosophy: How to Save Life on Earth (2021).*

Human purpose and the universal pursuit of ecstasy

It is possible that you like this book and that you thus start exploring what else I have written. So, I wanted to let you know that the only other book that you need is the book that I have just mentioned. You might discover that I have written two other books: *Human Purpose and the Universal Pursuit of Ecstasy (2019)*, and *Global Warming and Human Cosmic Purpose (2020)*. These two books are, in their entirety, included within *Mystical Environmental Philosophy: How to Save Life on Earth (2021)*, which is a large hardback.

Further information

You can find information about my philosophical project on my website:

www.drcphilosophy.com

You can also contact me via my website. It would be amazing to hear from you.

I hope that you have benefited from this book in some way.

Have a fabulous life.

Neil / Dr C

Sections

Milton Keynes UK
Ingram Content Group UK Ltd.
UKHW021516070924
447942UK00002B/25